CW00539352

101 Brockbank CARTOONS

Haynes Publishing

101 Brockbank CARTOONS

FOREWORD BY QUENTIN BLAKE

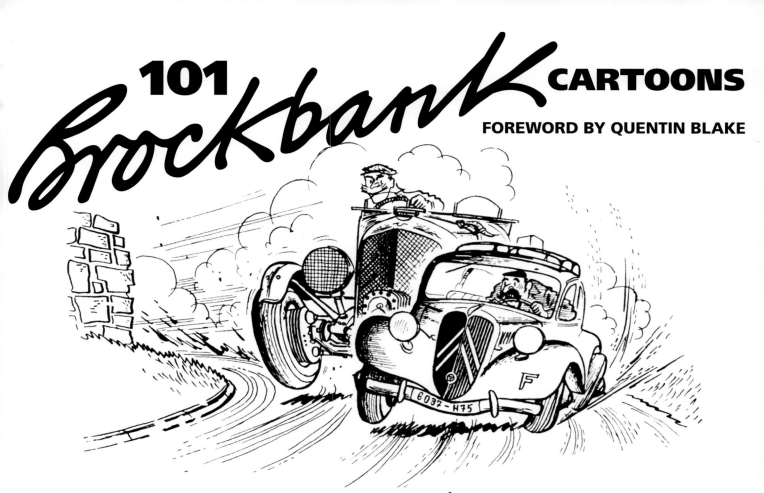

CITRON PRESSÉ

© The Brockbank Partnership

All rights reserved. No part of this publication may be reproduced, stored in a retrieval system or transmitted, in any form or by any means, electronic, mechanical, photocopying, recording or otherwise, without prior permission in writing from the publisher.

First published in September 2008

A catalogue record for this book is available from the British Library

ISBN 978 1 84425 647 1

Library of Congress catalog card no 2008933794

Haynes North America Inc., 861 Lawrence Drive, Newbury Park, California 91320, USA.

Published by Haynes Publishing, Sparkford, Yeovil, Somerset BA22 7JJ, UK.

Tel: 01963 442030 Fax: 01963 440001
Int. tel: +44 1963 442030 Int. fax: +44 1963 440001
E-mail: sales@haynes.co.uk
Website: www.haynes.co.uk

Printed and bound in Britain by J. H. Haynes & Co. Ltd, Sparkford

All cartoons copyright The Brockbank Partnership, many of which are available as prints. For more information and sales, visit www.russellbrockbank.co.uk or email Chris Ellis at suechrisellis@btinternet.com

Contents

Foreword

BY QUENTIN BLAKE

It's a real pleasure to me to be able to write some words at the beginning of this collection of drawings by Russell Brockbank. When we first met – I was about to write '50 years ago' but I realise it's actually nearer 60 – we were both, in our different ways, beginners. When as a teenage schoolboy I entered for the first time those impressive premises of Punch Office in Bouverie Street, Russell had just seated himself in the art editor's chair. His generosity towards a young hopeful was characteristic of him, and I still have that first formal letter of acceptance with, on the bottom, in what was to become familiar handwriting, the words 'congratulations to the youngest contributor'.

A generosity towards my awkward early efforts was all the more marked when you consider by contrast the skills that he brought into the field. He could give you a comedy situation that was not detracted from but authenticated by a wealth of assured vehicular information. I look again and see that the 'Citron Pressé' is in beautiful perspective, and that evocative French road is also in beautiful perspective; one doesn't appreciate these things any less over the years. Perhaps at that time there remained still some air of romance and adventure in motoring that it's less easy to find now, so that Russell was in the driving seat of his drawing board at a time, as Evelyn Waugh put it, 'when the going was good'. And what an excellent man at the wheel!

Quentin Blake

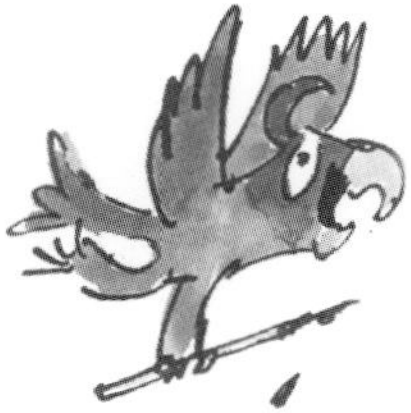

Introduction

BY SUE & ROGER BROCKBANK

Those who remember the fifties, sixties and seventies will be familiar with the cartoons of Russell Brockbank. Happily a new generation is showing an eager enthusiasm for his work and this book warmly welcomes these new fans. Russell enjoyed the company of the young and was always interested and encouraging of their ideas. He was blessed with many talents, one of which was an open-mindedness to all ages and backgrounds. and this is reflected in his drawings.

'Brock', as he was affectionately known, was born in Canada in 1913. As family folklore reflects, his mother, although living in the USA, made a dash in a thunderstorm over the bridge at Niagara so that her second son was born on British Empire soil! A happy childhood and adolescence followed. Brock started drawing cars from the age of four, and playing cricket and ice hockey in his teens.

With the Depression of 1929, the family returned to England and Brock enrolled at the Chelsea School of Art. Unfortunately while there his love of racing cars was his downfall. At Brooklands he was caught on camera helping a driver out of a burning car and his father spotted him on *Pathé News*! He was immediately removed from Chelsea and taken into his father's industrial ceramics firm.

He continued drawing and had his first break when he sold five drawings to Prince Bira, the famous racing driver. He asked for a fee of £5 but was amazed to get £5 for each drawing – £25 in total. That was a few week's wages in those days.

He had become a professional artist and was soon contributing to *Punch*, *Lilliput* and *Speed* magazines, gradually developing a unique technique and ability to combine precise accuracy of detail with wildly expressive animation, famously portrayed in his Blower Bentley illustrations such as 'Citron Pressé'.

He served in the Royal Navy throughout the Second World War, to VE Day and beyond to VJ Day, and managed to continue drawing for *The Aeroplane* and *Flight* magazines, amongst others. In 1949 he was appointed Art Editor of *Punch*, where he introduced a weekly change of the front cover into colour – a controversial action for a traditional publication – and encouraged young artists such as Ronald Searle, Norman Thelwell, Larry, André François and Quentin Blake.

For *The Motor* magazine, Brock created a weekly strip cartoon featuring 'Major Upsett' and his clapped-out Austin 8 Tourer. Brock based this character on a man he observed in a pub, and he descibed him as having 'a fiery eye, nose pocked like the surface of the moon, the twitch of his outmoded moustache which in moments of stress made him rattle all over'. Major Upsett's escapades and forthright opinions reflected the many social changes of the time. Even grown men and their sons fought over their copy to find out what the Major had been up to each week.

Brock loved to drive fast whenever he had the opportunity. He was very proud of his Advanced Driver's badge, and his examiner apparently remarked that he had never been driven so skilfully and fast around Brands Hatch.

He owned a Porsche 356, an Alfa Romeo 1750 GT and a Mini-Cooper. He took the Mini-Cooper to the USA, where people laughed at the little car, until Brock put his foot down and accelerated past the lumbering Chryslers and Chevrolets – and was promptly caught for speeding. But the American cop just grinned at the audaciousness of the Mini-Cooper and Brock was let off.

He loved to go to Silverstone, Goodwood, Rheims and Monza. He would quietly observe the racing teams at work, sketching and catching the ripe exchanges between drivers, mechanics and owners – a selection of this work can be found inside this book. He particularly enjoyed the Le Mans 24-hour race that took him away from home for a week every year, always mystifying his wife Eileen! He came home triumphant one year with a French road sign that said 'Man at Work' and proudly nailed it to the outside of his studio – no questions were asked!

Brock always said he was the luckiest of men, for he loved his job. Although motoring and the motor car inspired much of his work, he was also at home with aircraft, ships, space-age subjects and every imaginable domestic situation. His work was characterised by a wonderful sense of humour and an eye for the bizarre situation that 'might just happen'. He poked gentle fun but never caused offence. He was the kindest of men. Sadly he died at the early age of 66, but he has left behind a wonderful legacy.

In 2006 the family of Brockbank decided to revive his work, creating a website showing a selection of his drawings. Many requests for a new book have been made and we are grateful to Haynes Publishing for making this happen and to Quentin Blake for honouring the book with a foreword.

We hope those who are new to Brockbank will enjoy this book as much as we have enjoyed putting together the 101 Brockbanks in it – and chuckling all the way.

Sue and Roger Backseat

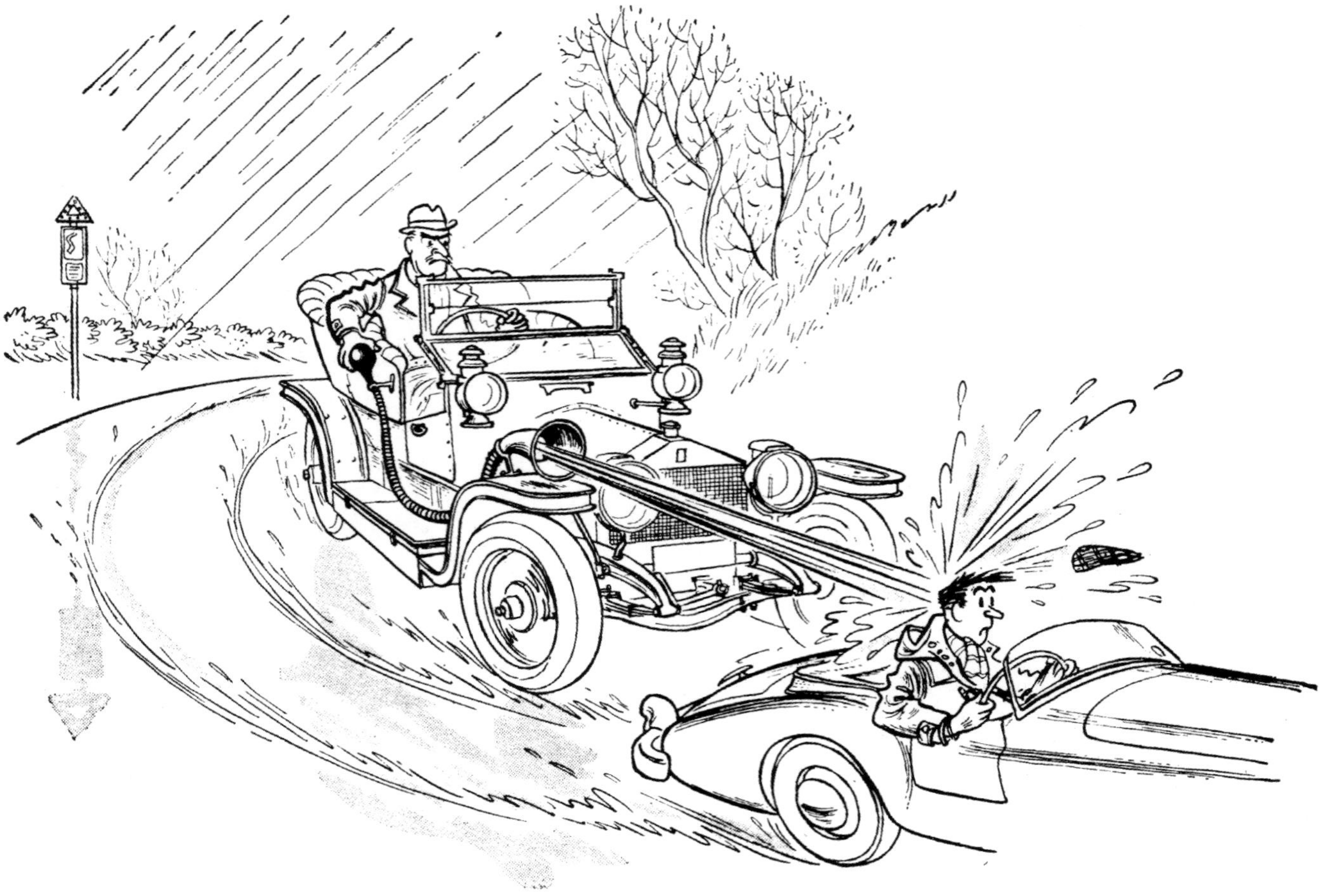

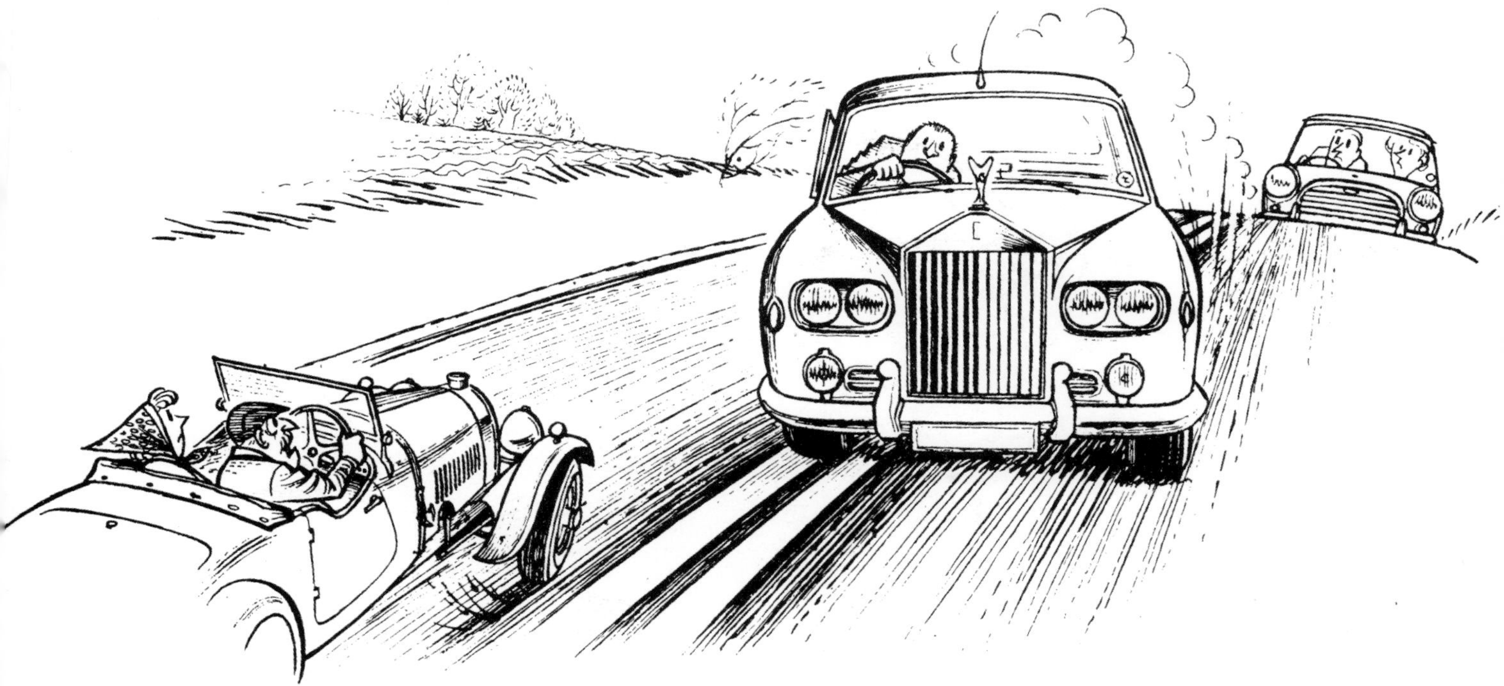

'A typical example of the money getting into the wrong hands.'

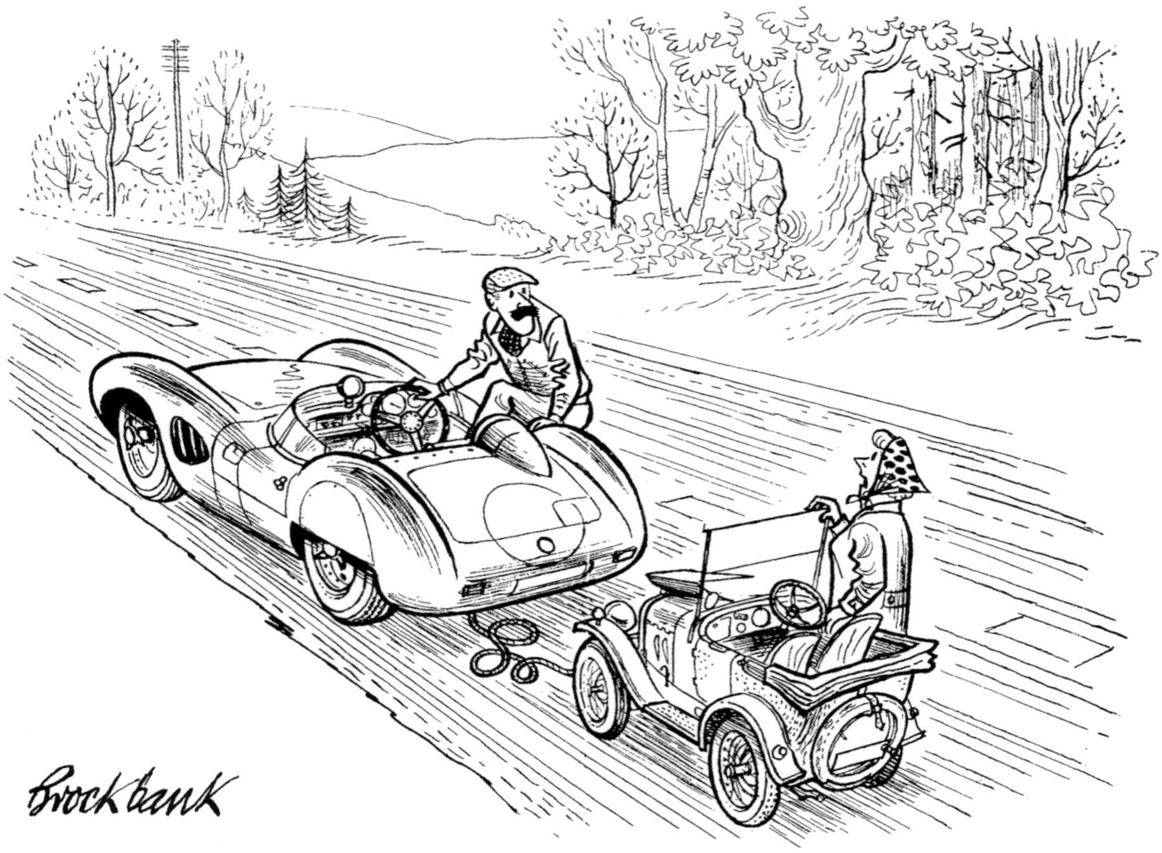
Brockbank

‘Do you promise to tow me at the speed to which I am accustomed?’

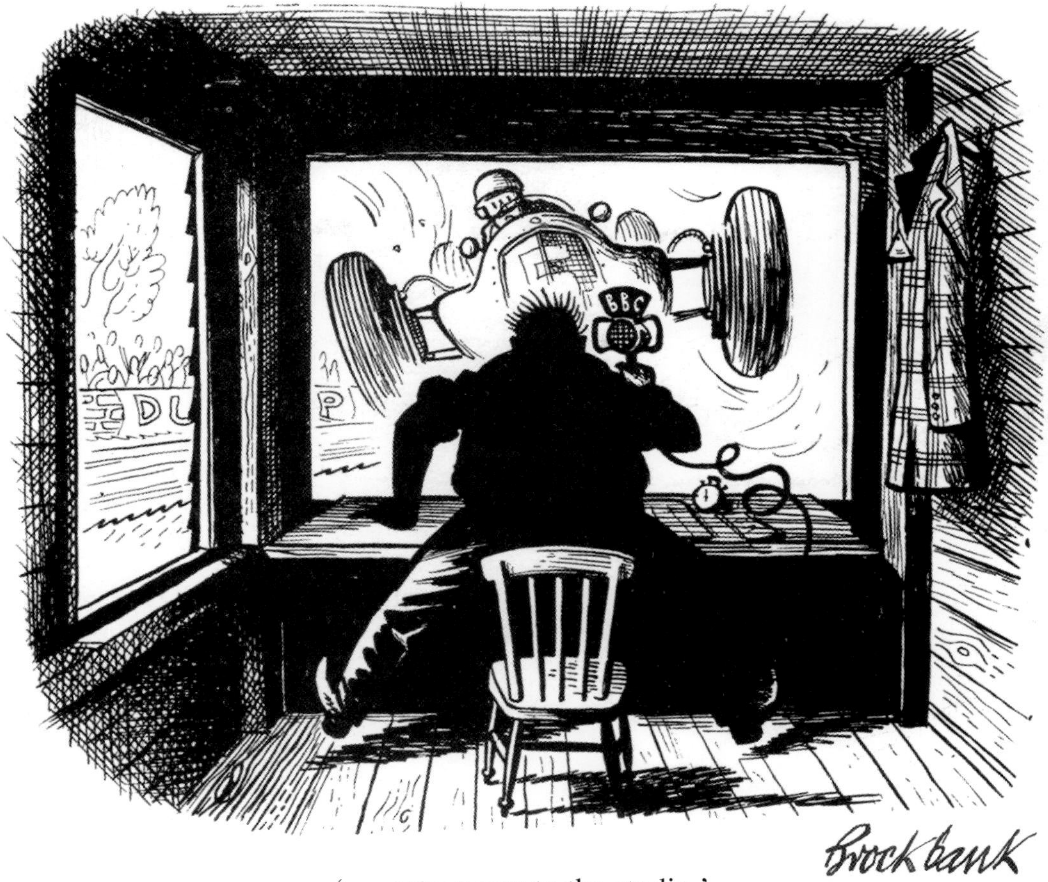
BBC
DU
P
Brockbank

'. . . return you to the studio.'

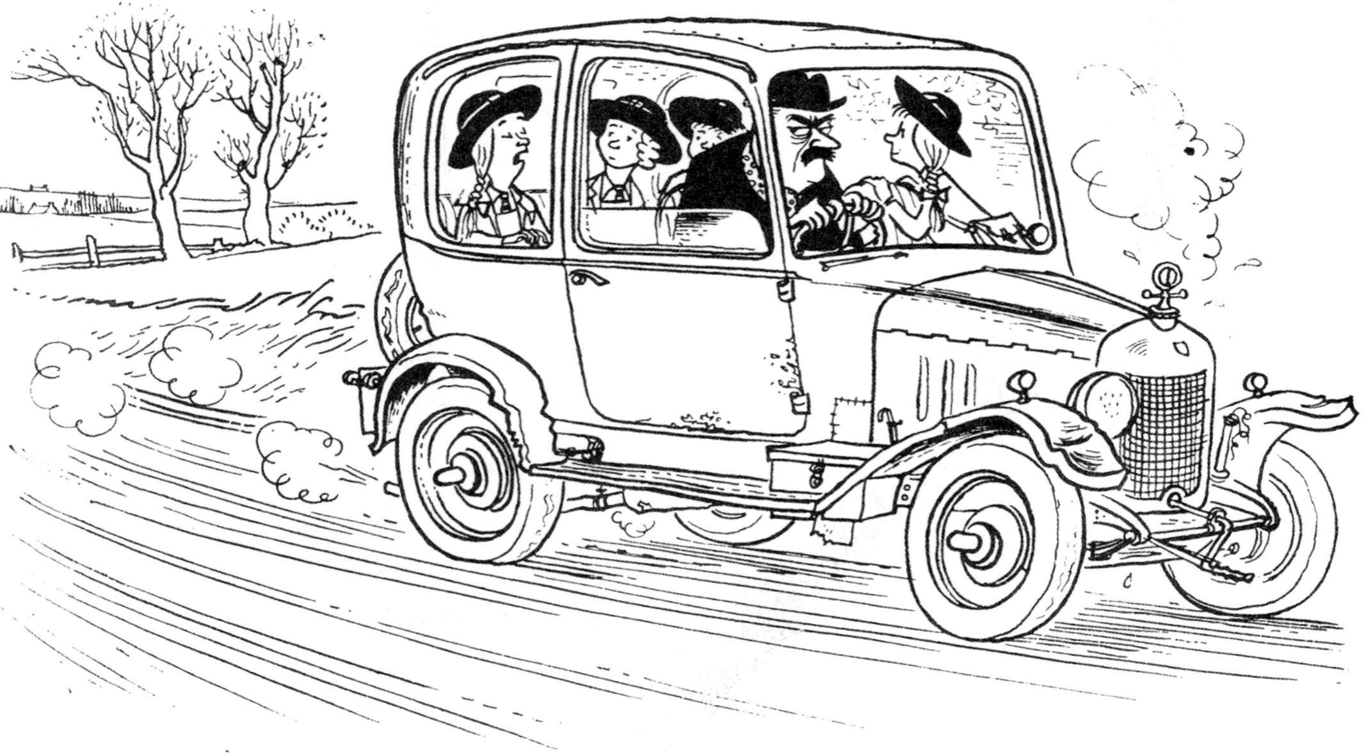

'My father's a racing driver.'

'Hop up man – it won't bite you.'

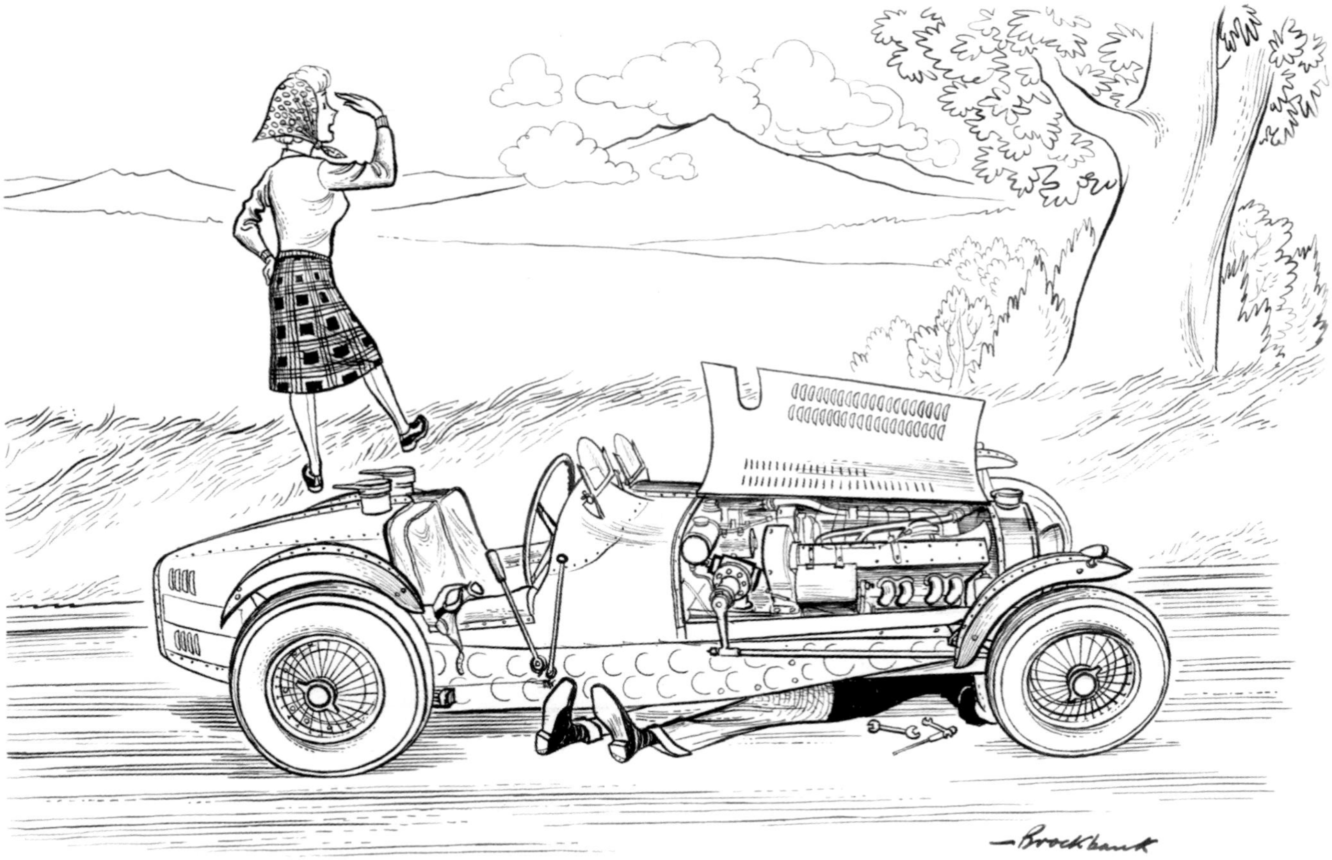
Brockbank

'First time in three days I've been able to take in the scenery'

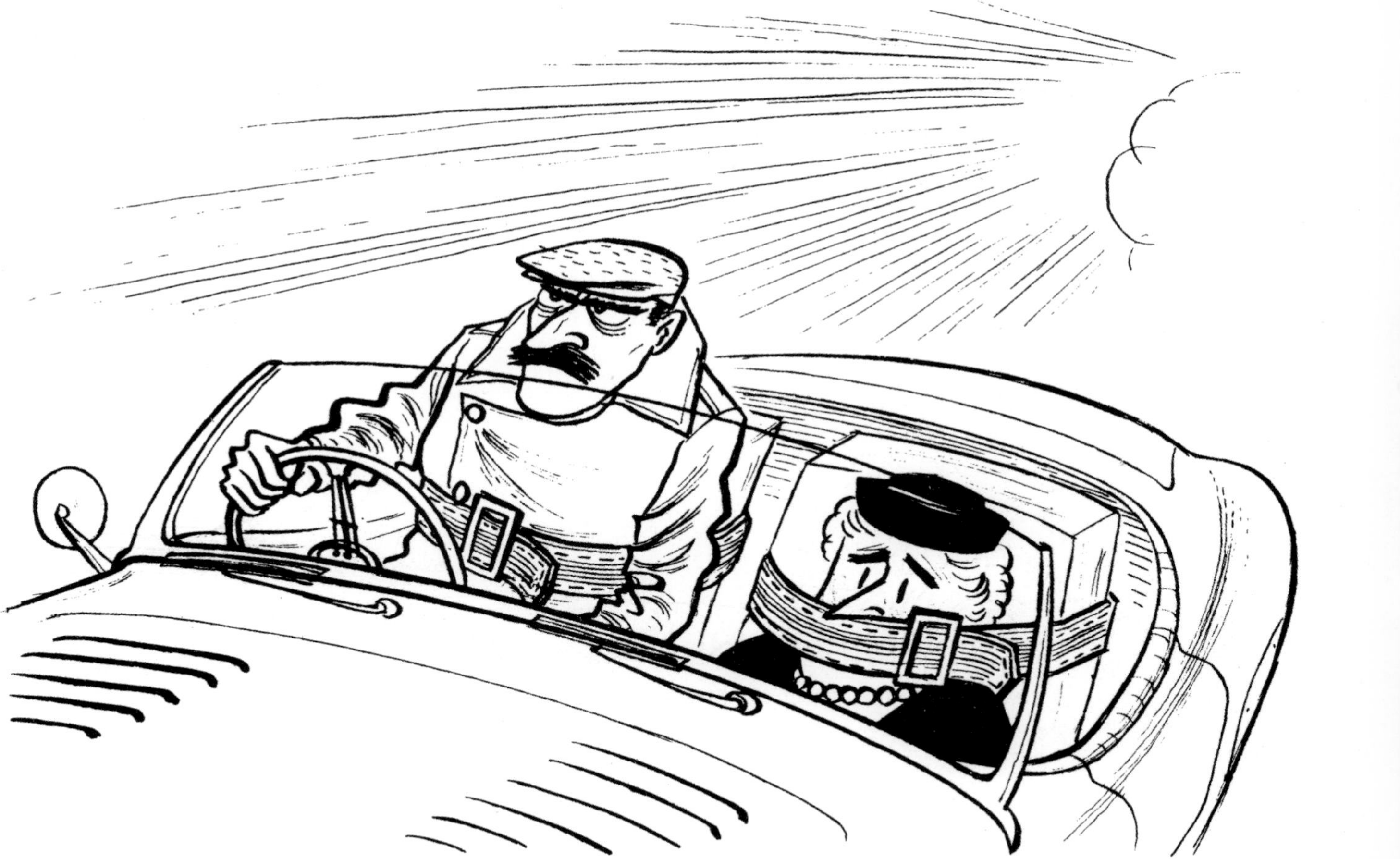

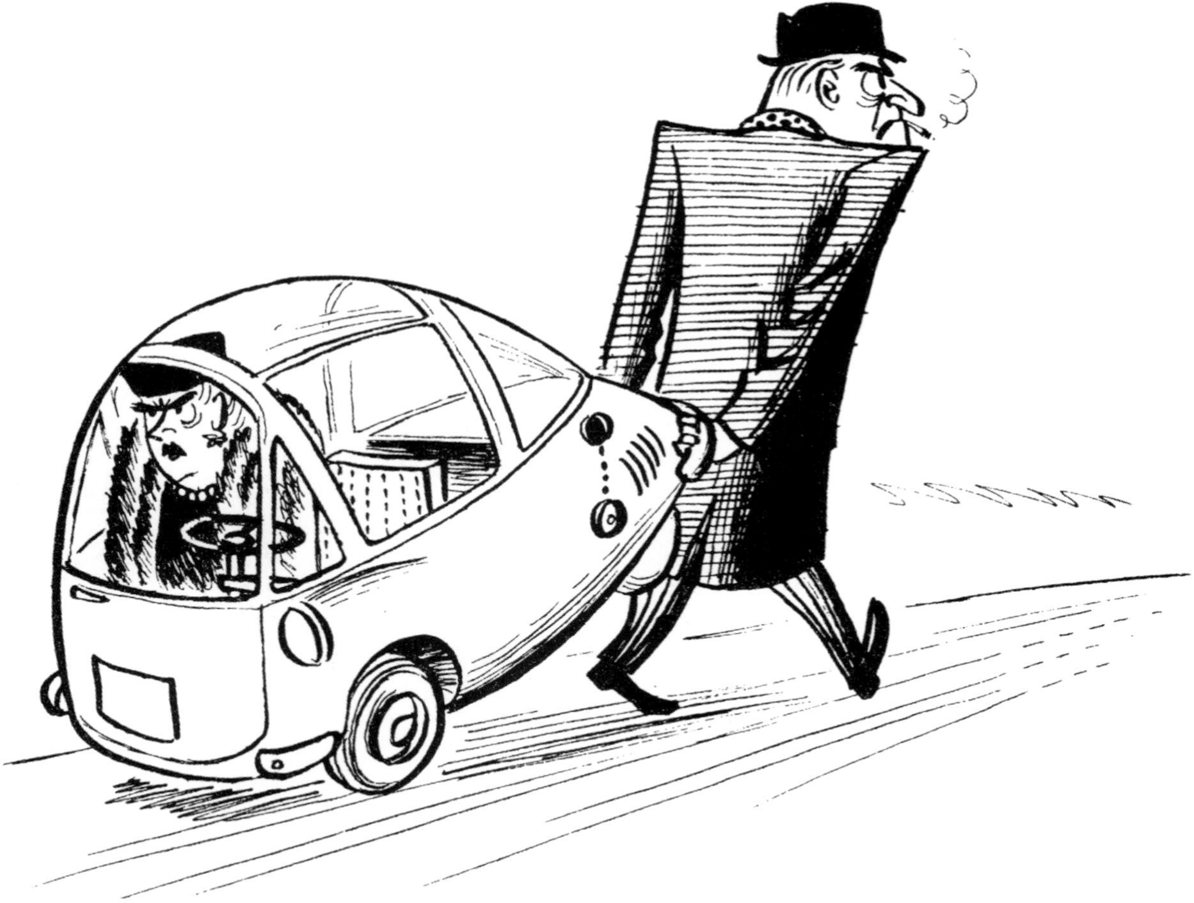

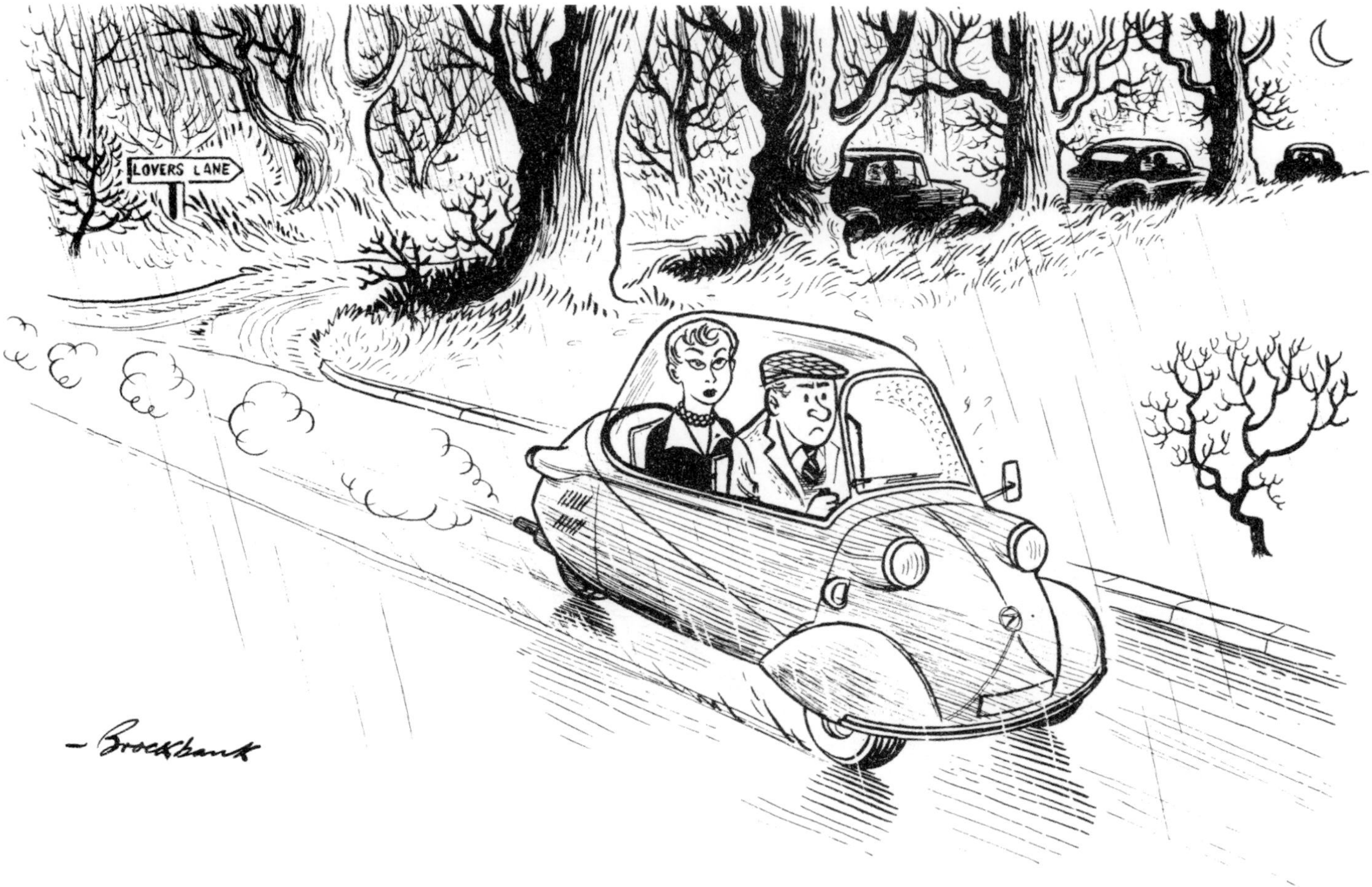
LOVERS LANE
Brockbank

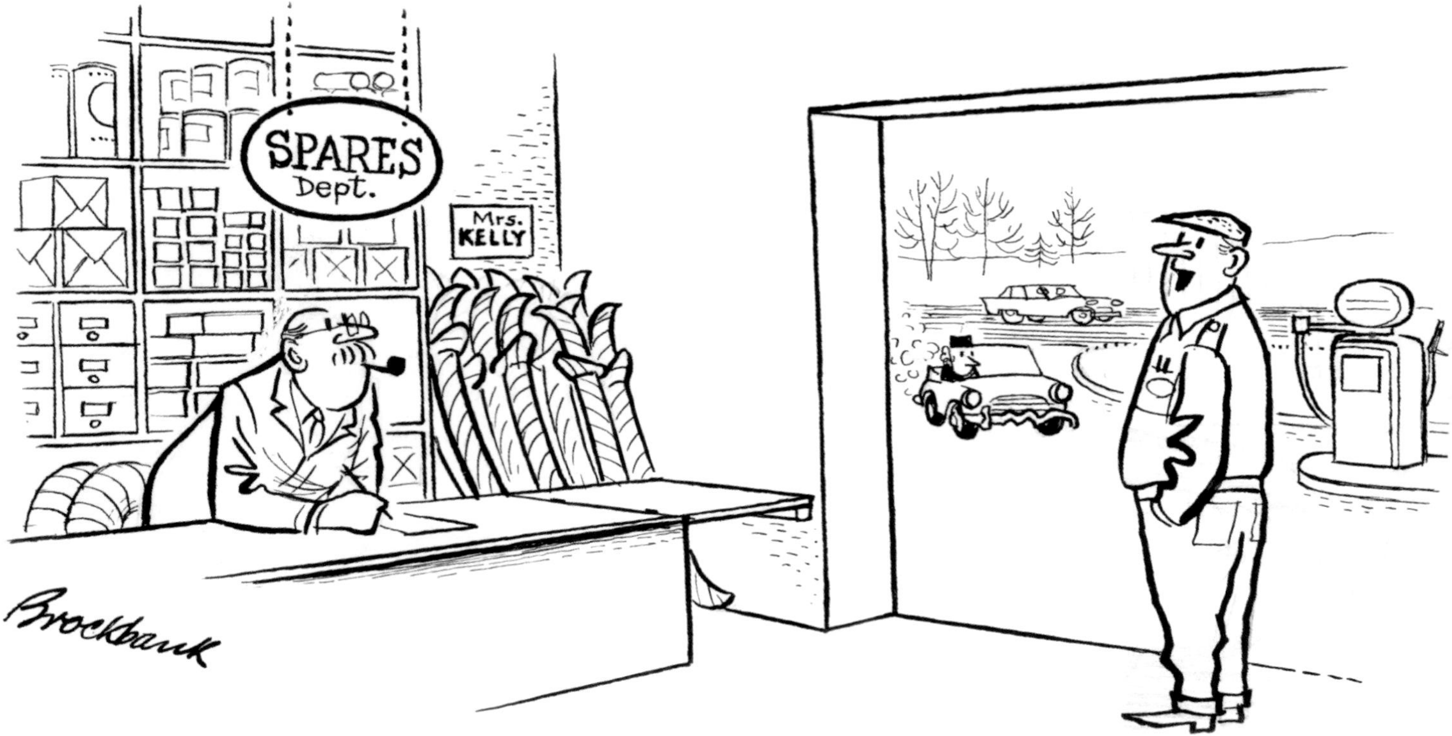
SPARES
Dept.
Mrs.
KELLY
Brockbank

'Mrs. Kelly's gatepost has done it again.'

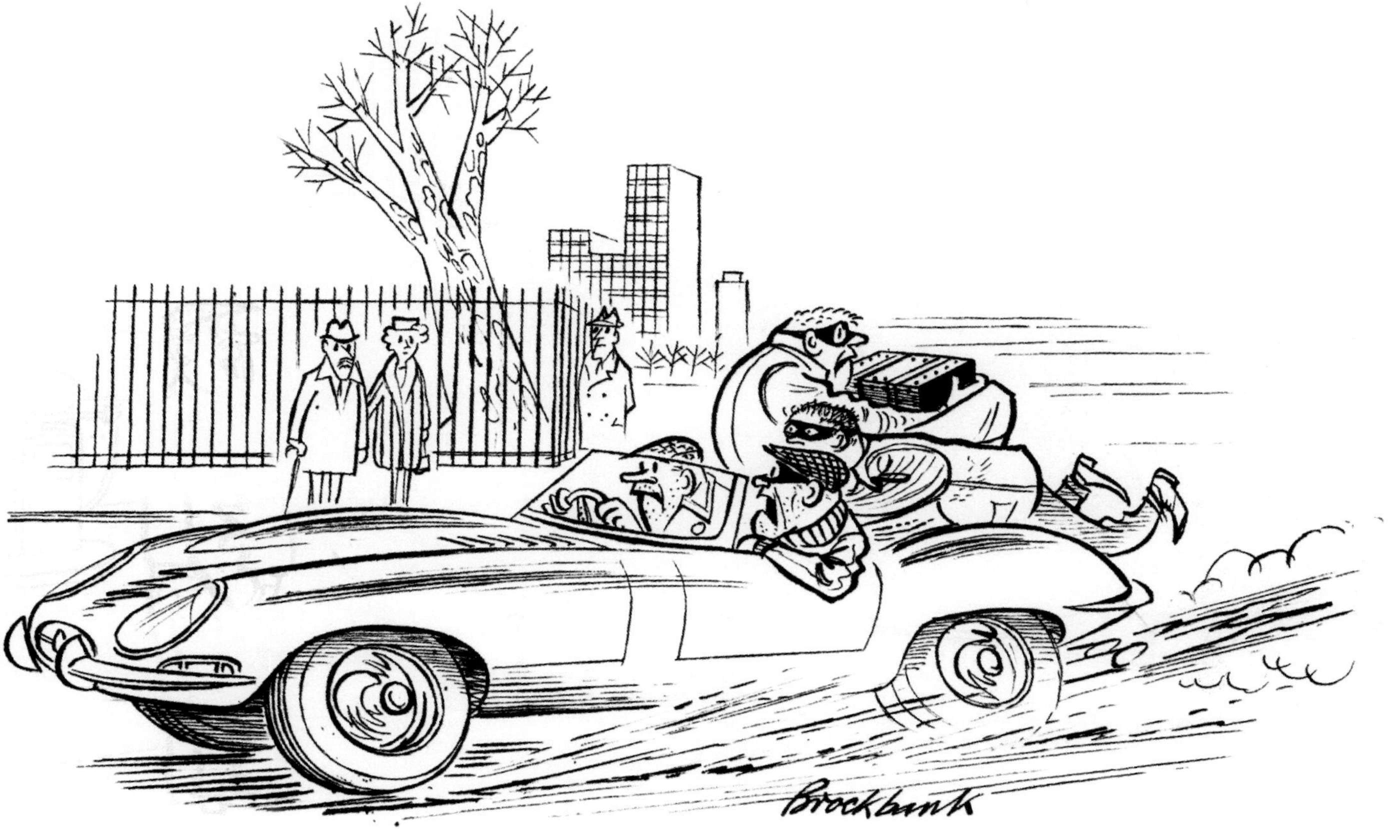
Brockbank

'When I said knock off a jag for the getaway, I didn't mean *this* model!'

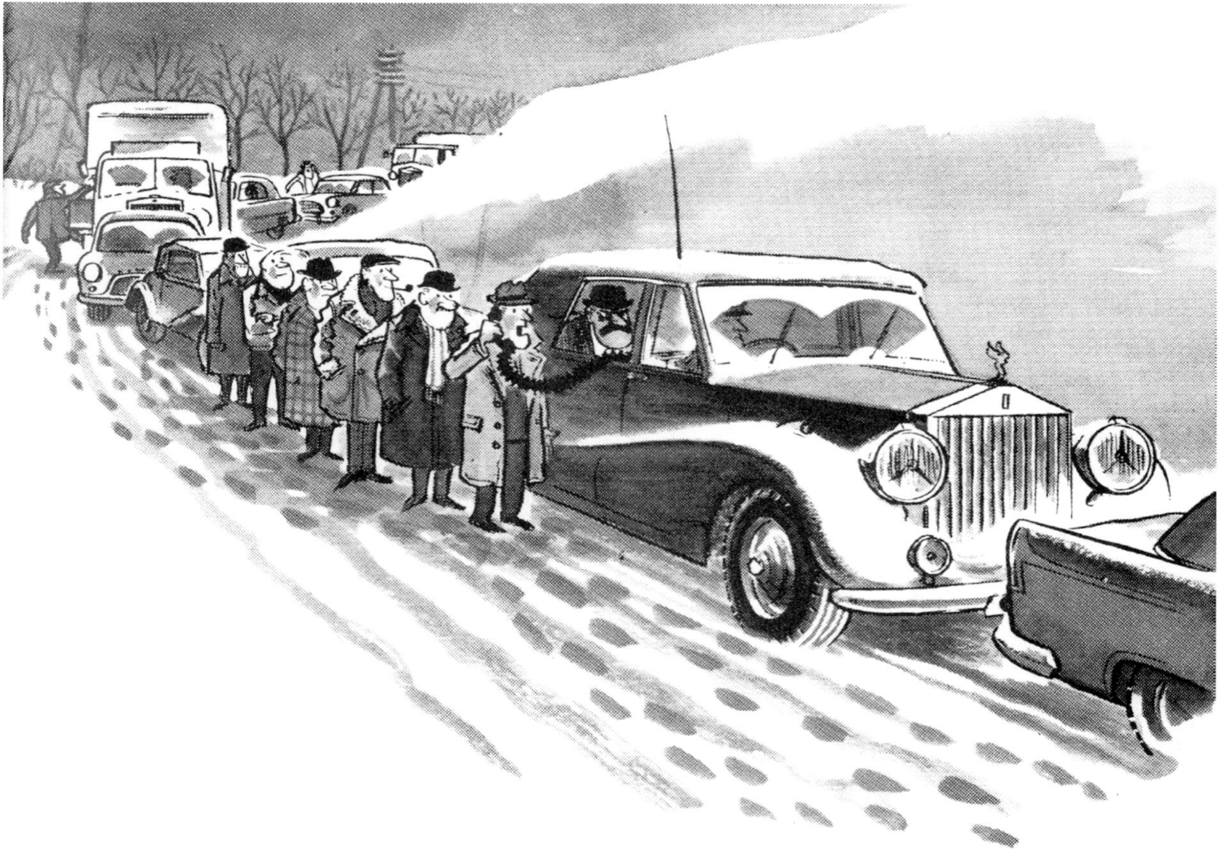

'I'm on the A30, on the wrong side of Salisbury and I look like being late for supper.'

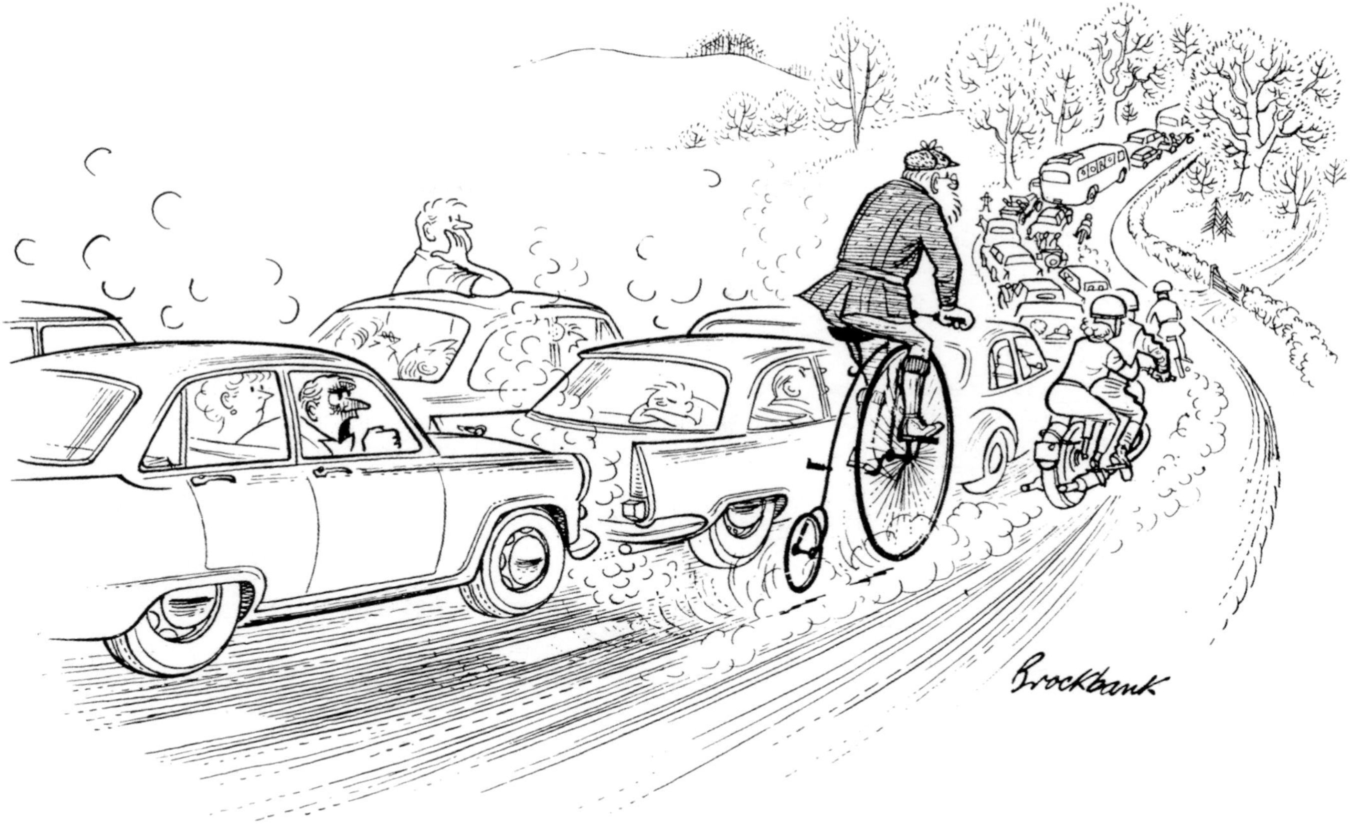
Brockbank

'THAT is the last straw!'

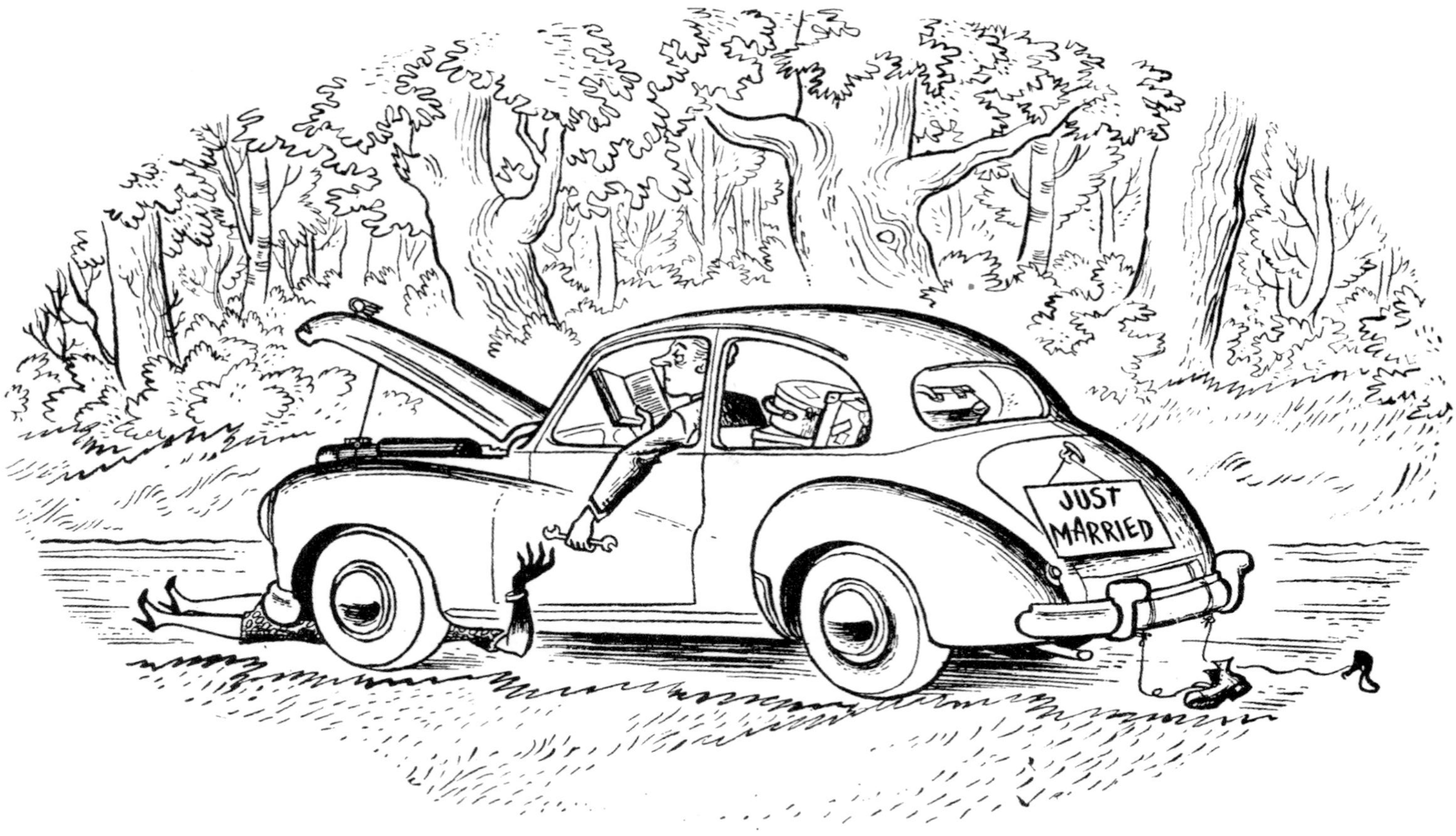
JUST MARRIED

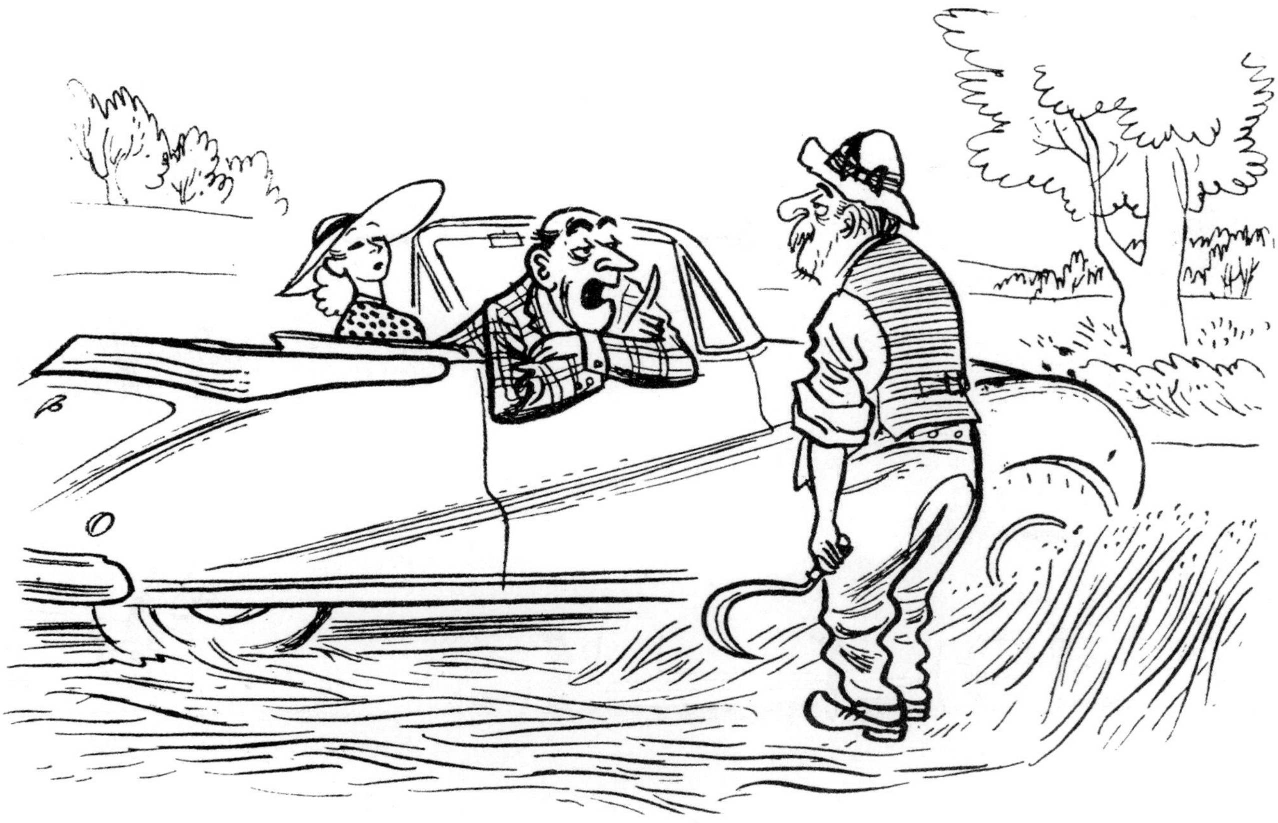

‘Now let’s take the hypothetical case of a person *not* wanting to go by way of the old stile, Seven-Acre Meadow and Bluebell Wood . . .’

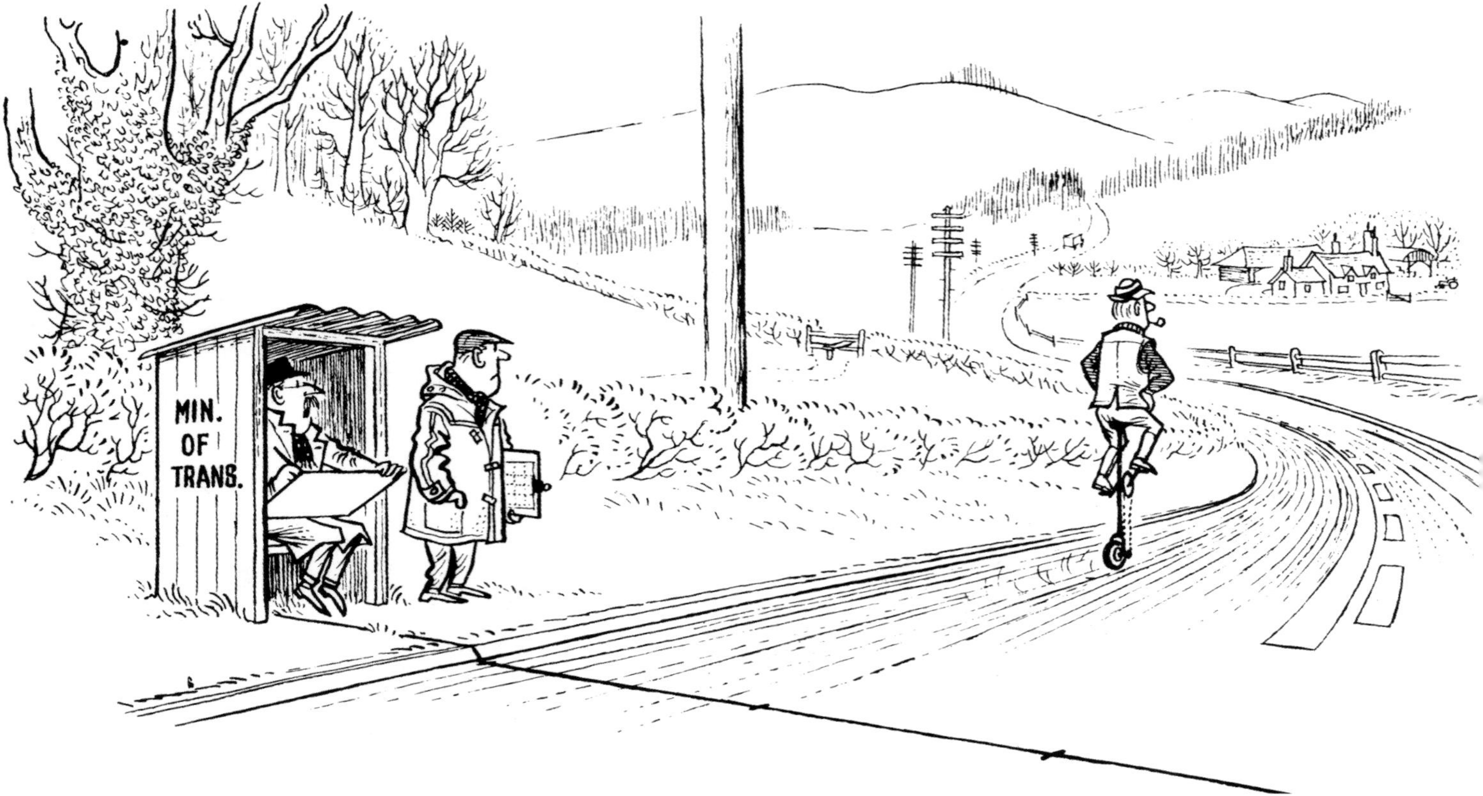
MIN.
OF
TRANS.

'That explains why we always end up with an *odd* number'

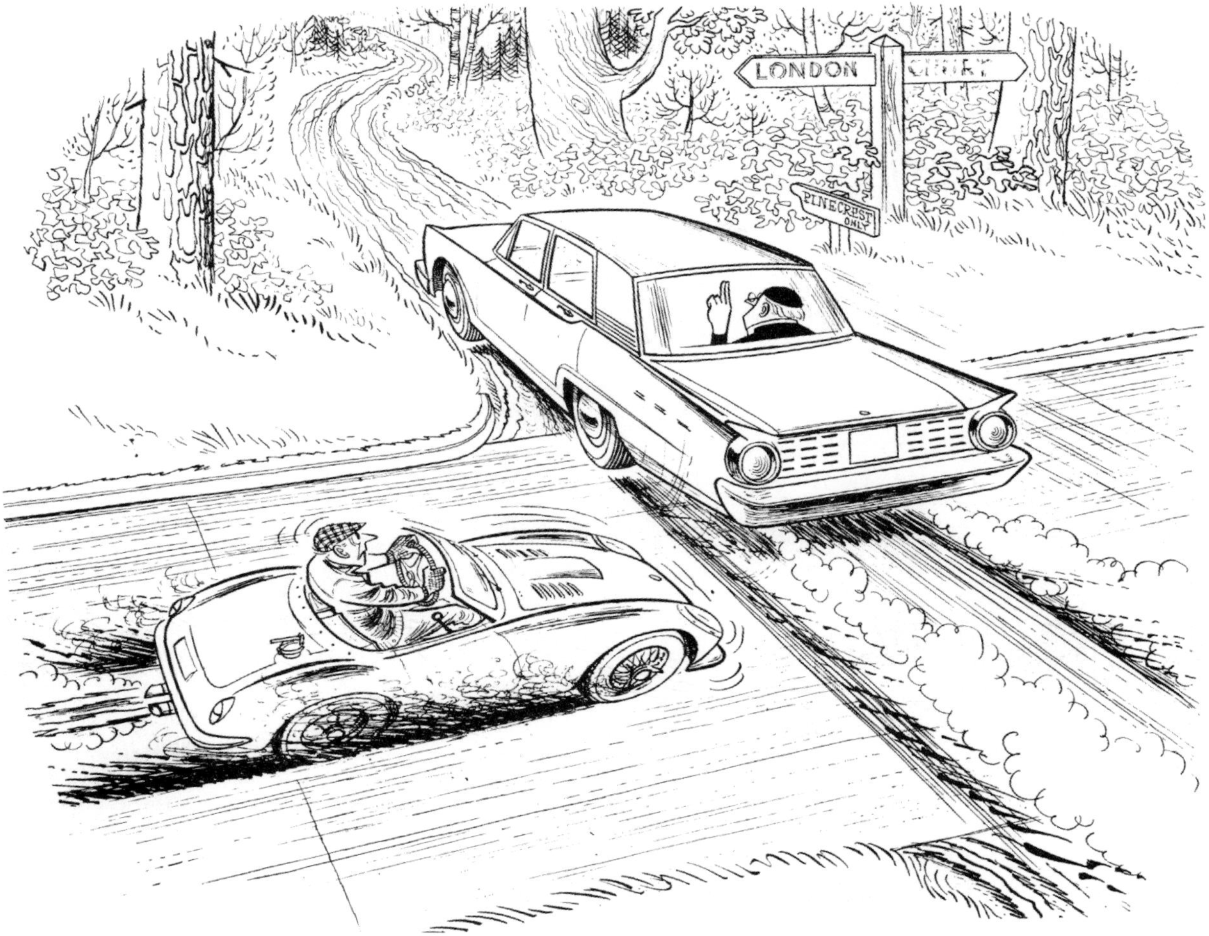
LONDON
PINECREST
ONLY

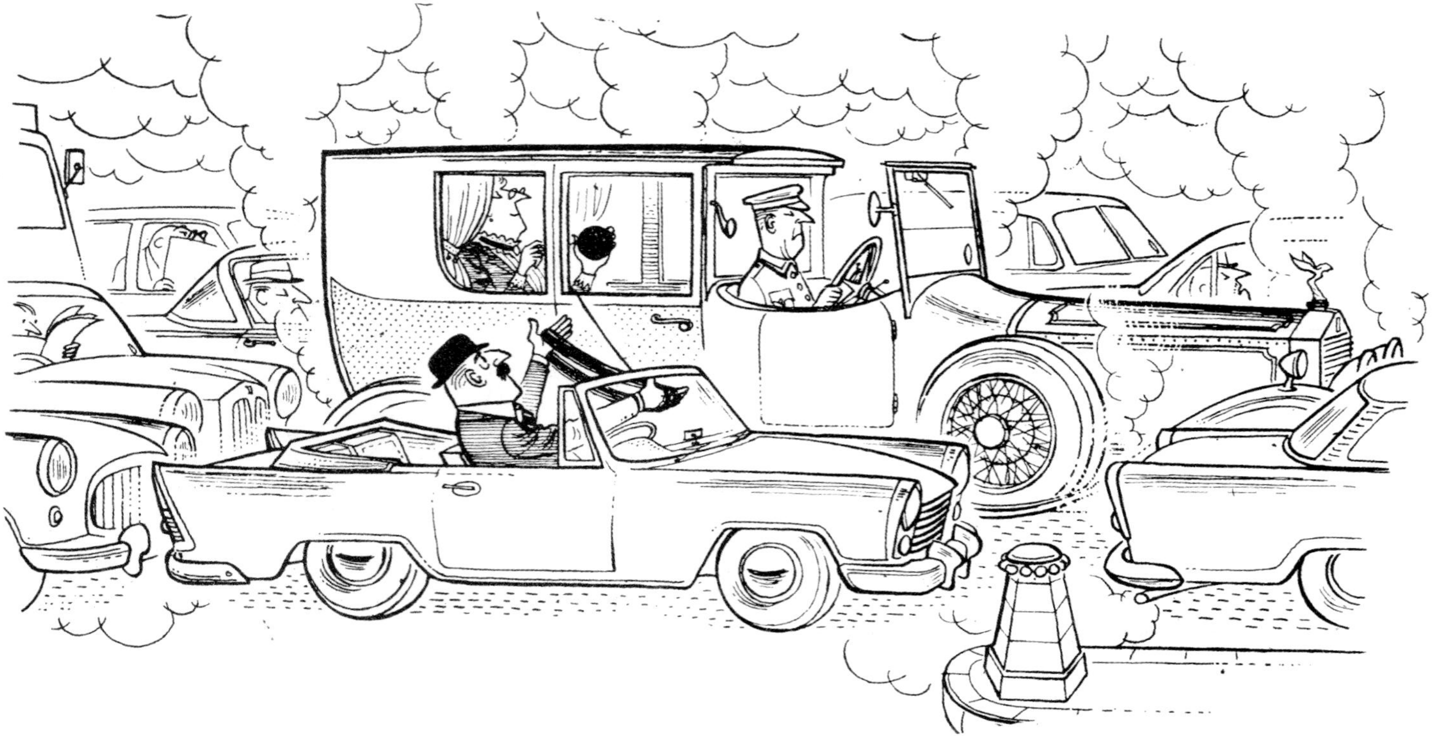

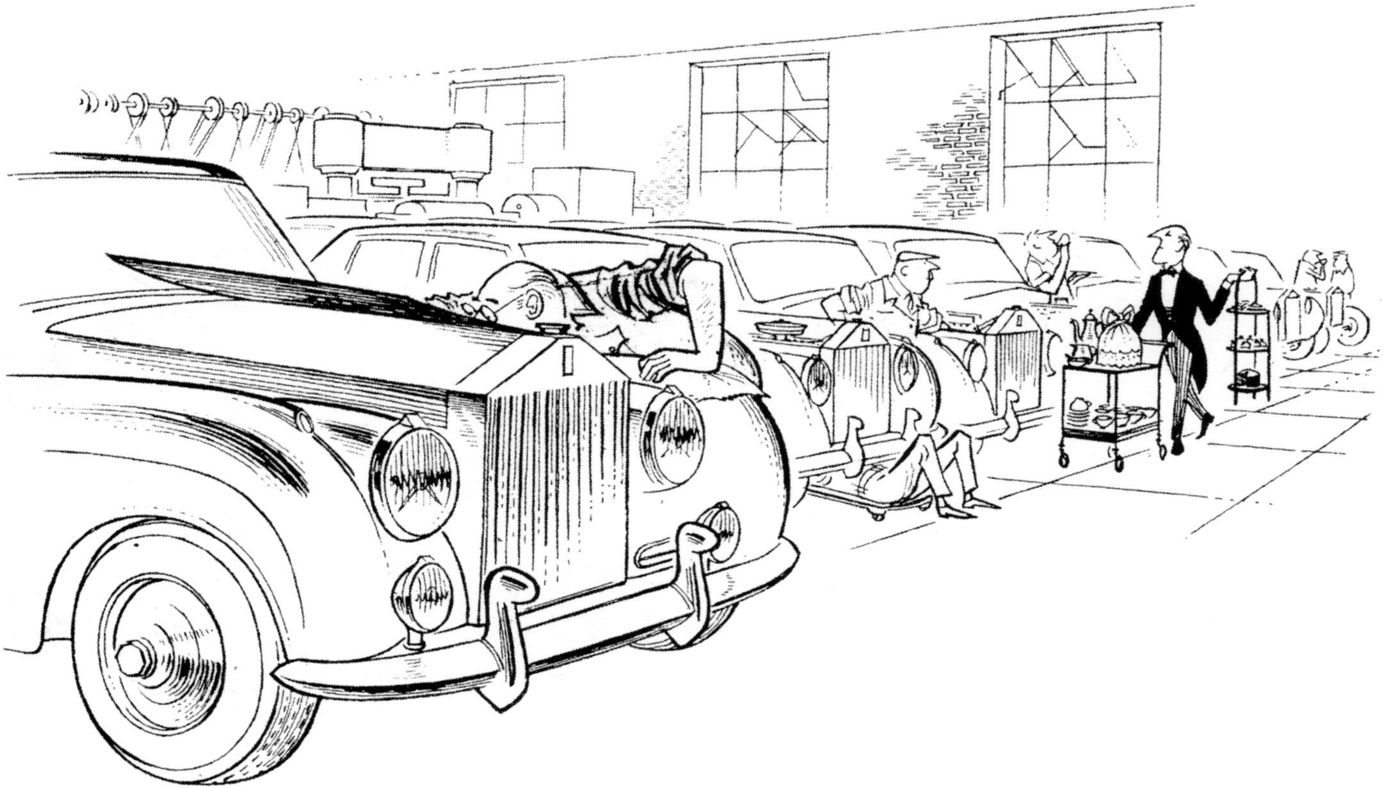

Tea time at Rolls-Royce

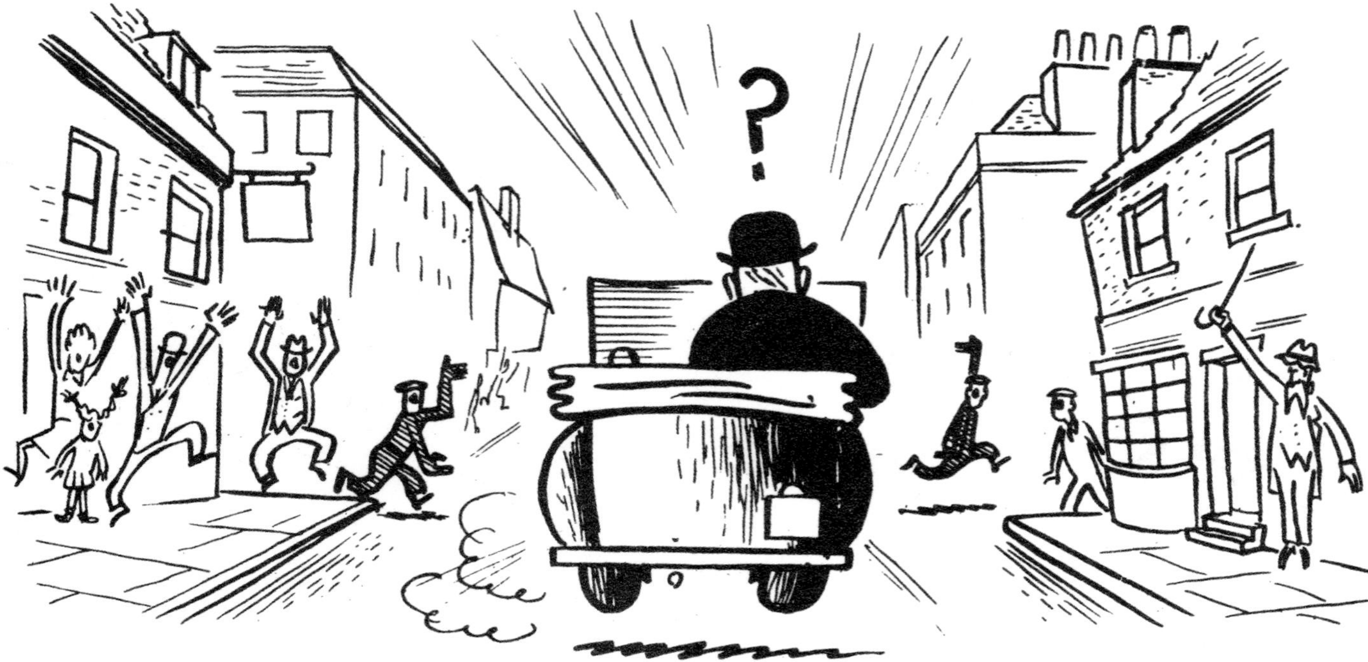
?

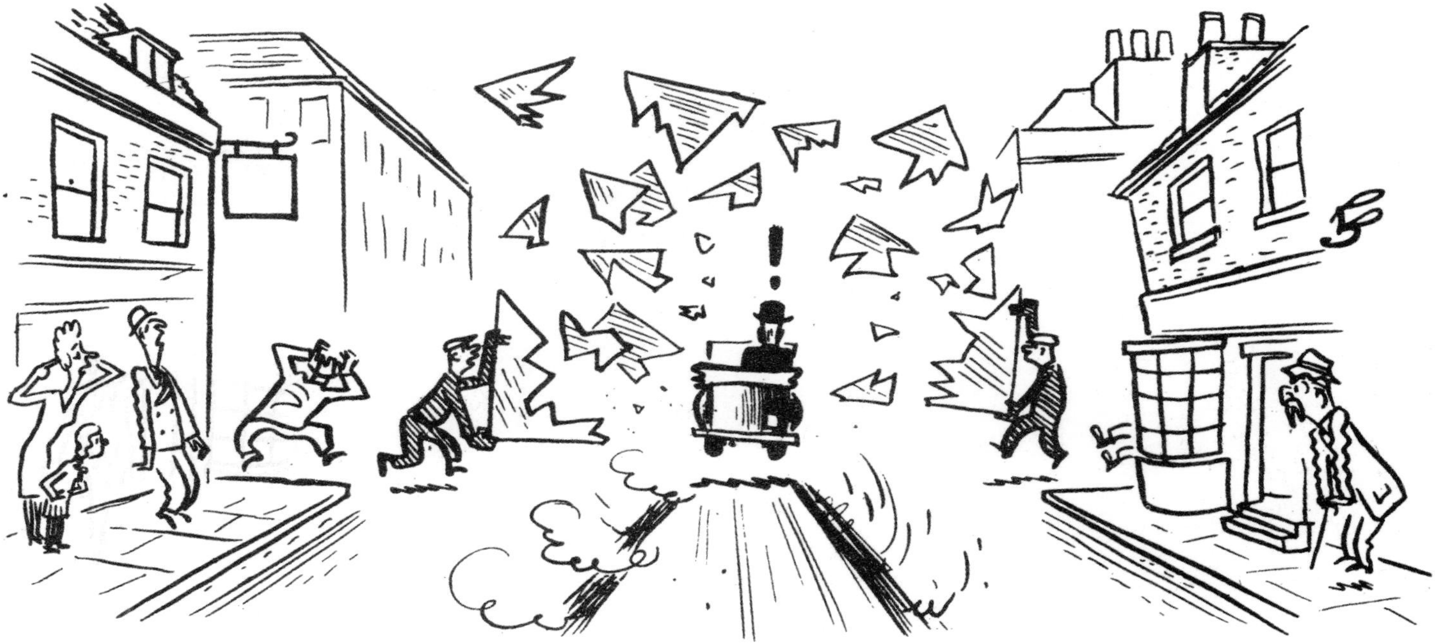

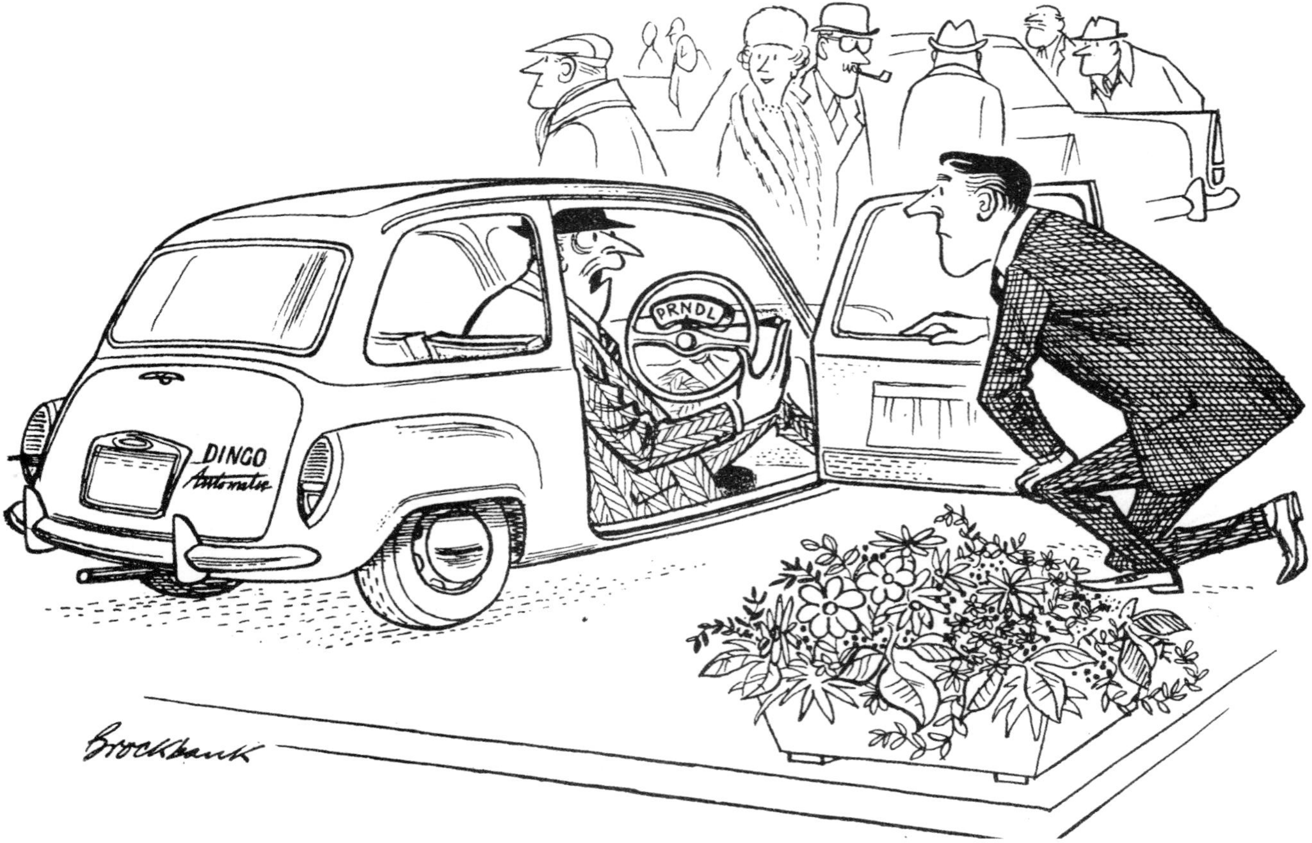
PRNDL
DINGO
Automatic
Brockbank

'What the hell is the PRNDL?'

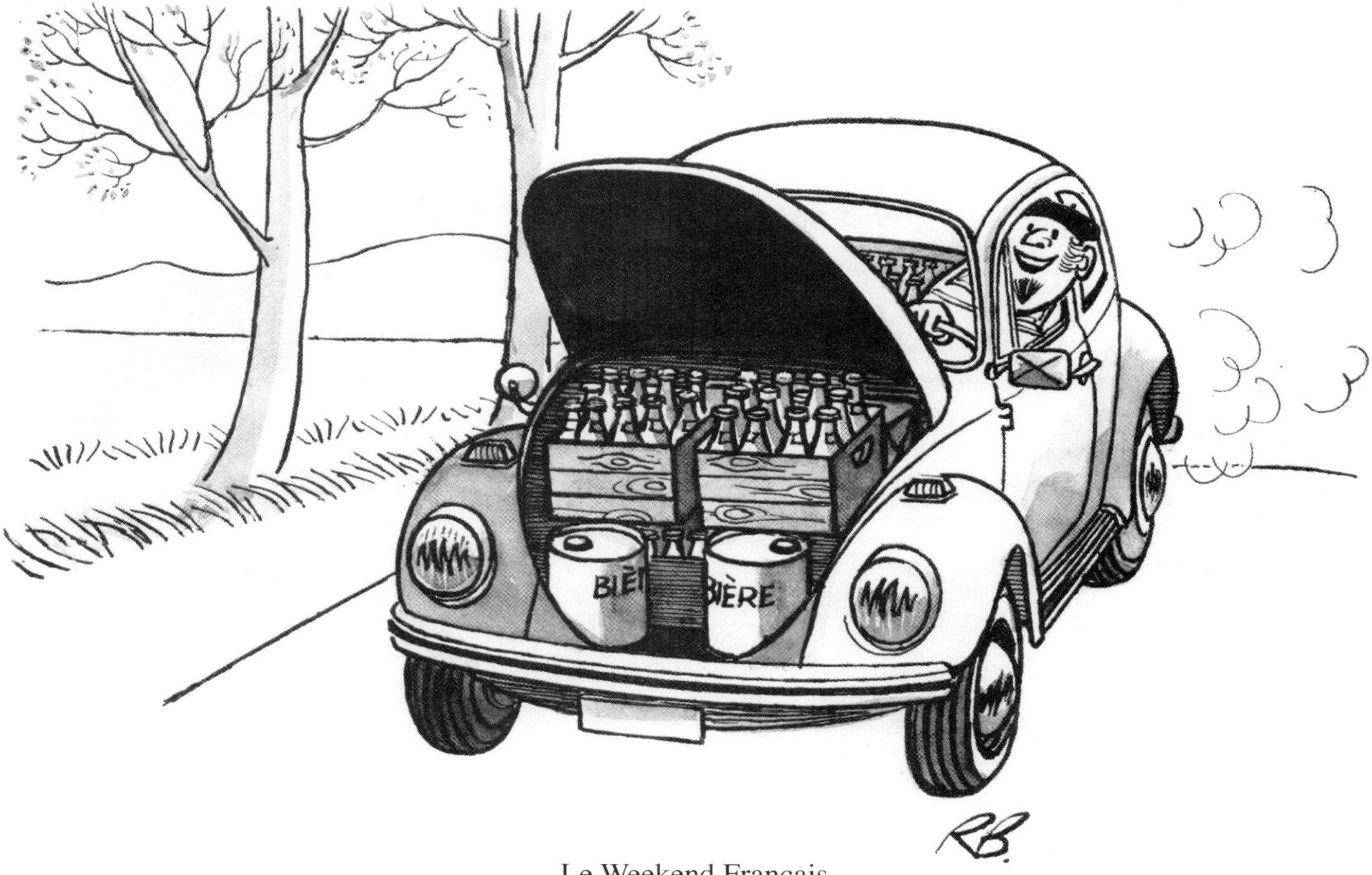
BIÈRE
BIÈ
RB.

Le Weekend Francais

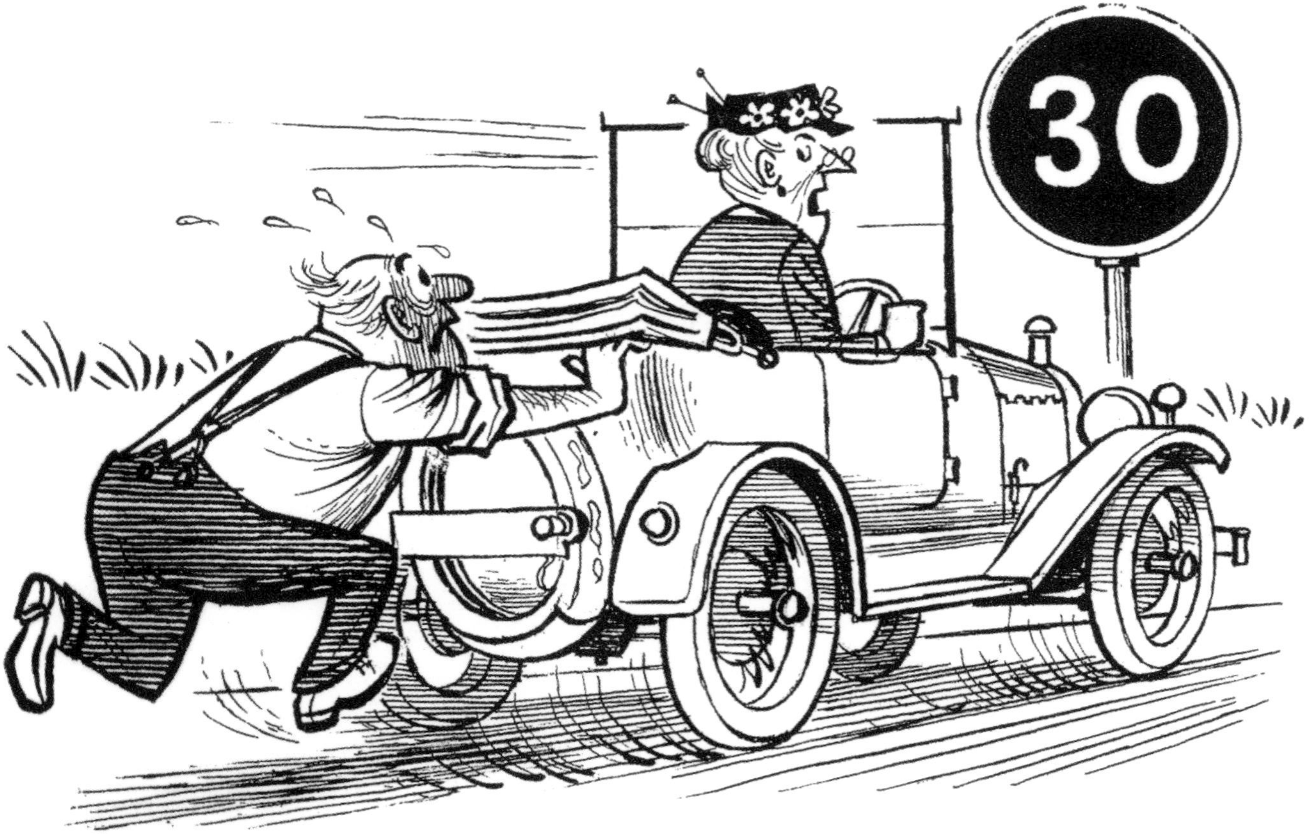
30

‘You can slow down now, Edgar.’

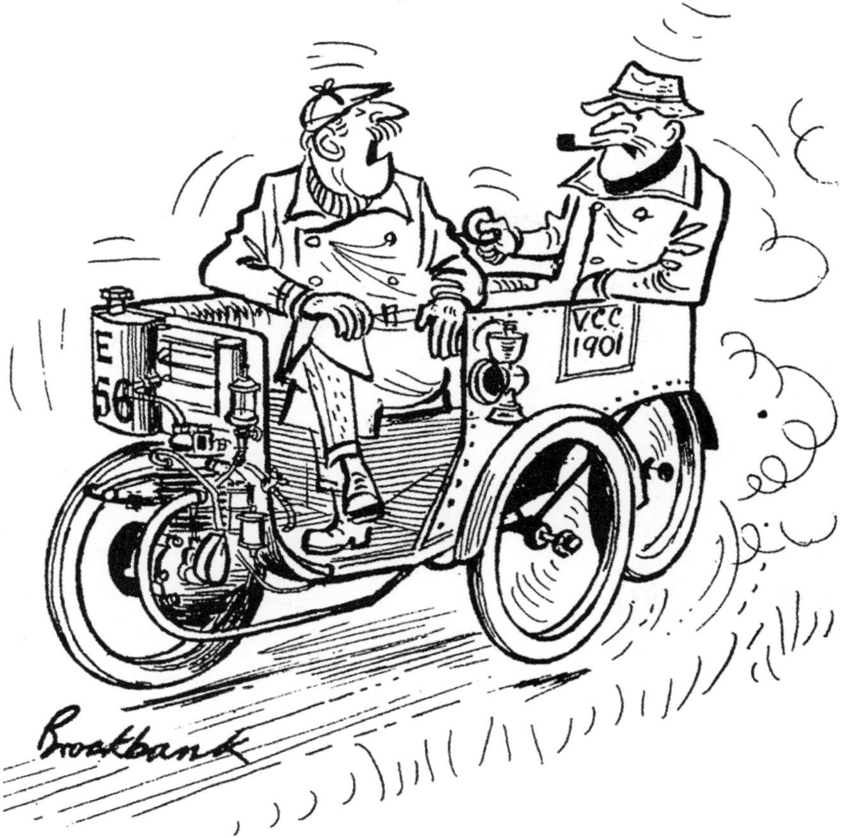
E
56
V.C.C.
1901
Brockbank

'And all they do is laugh'

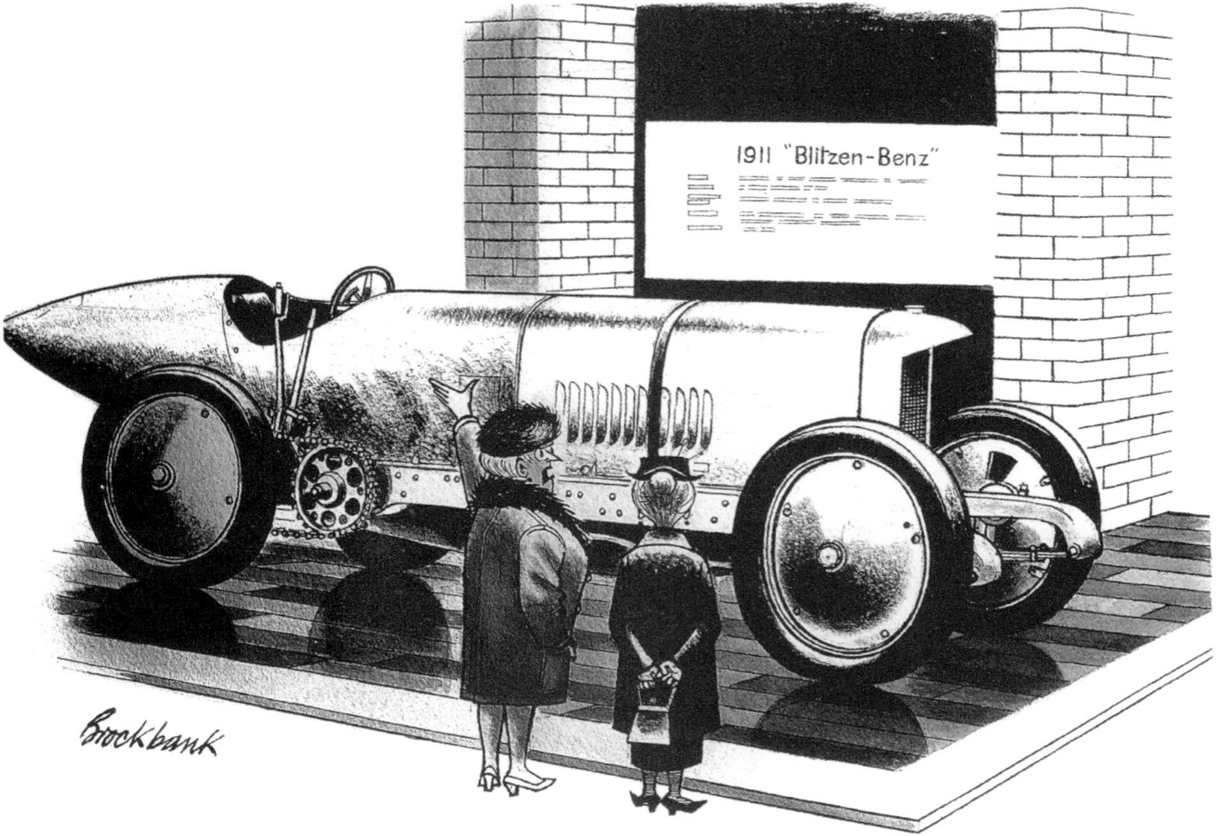
1911 "Blitzen-Benz"
Brockbank

'200 horsepower, all for one selfish brute who never took his wife anywhere'

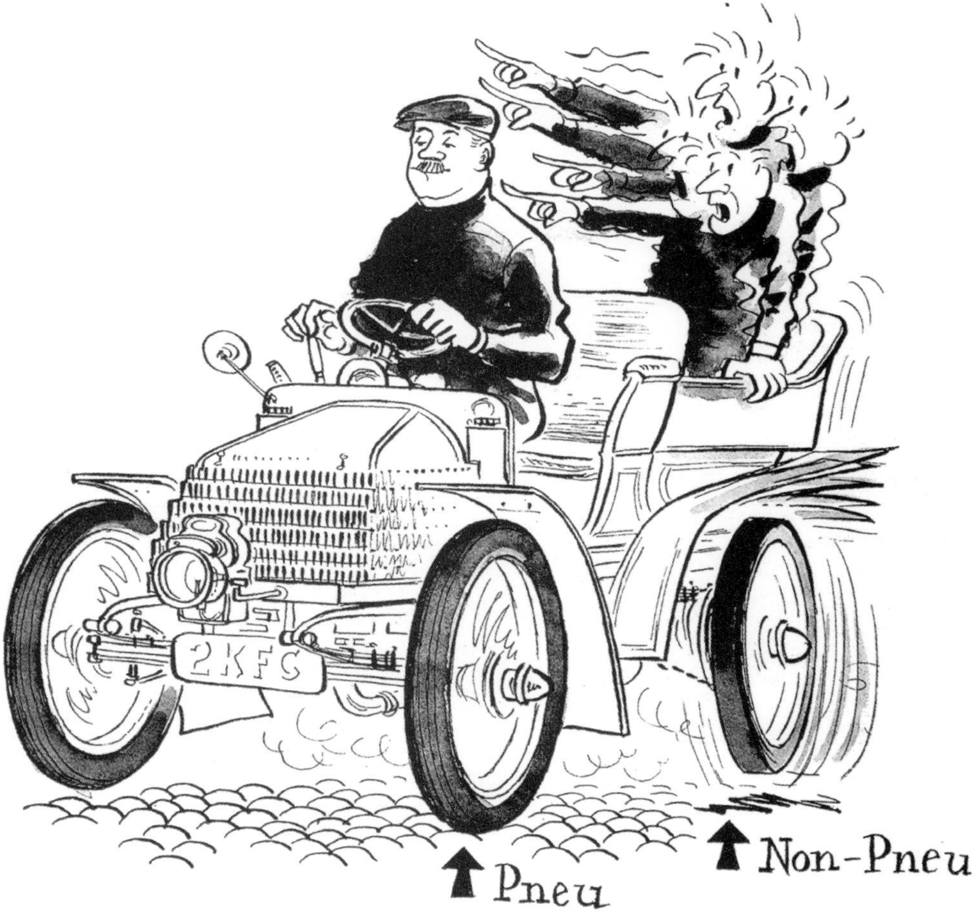
2KFS
Pneu
Non-Pneu

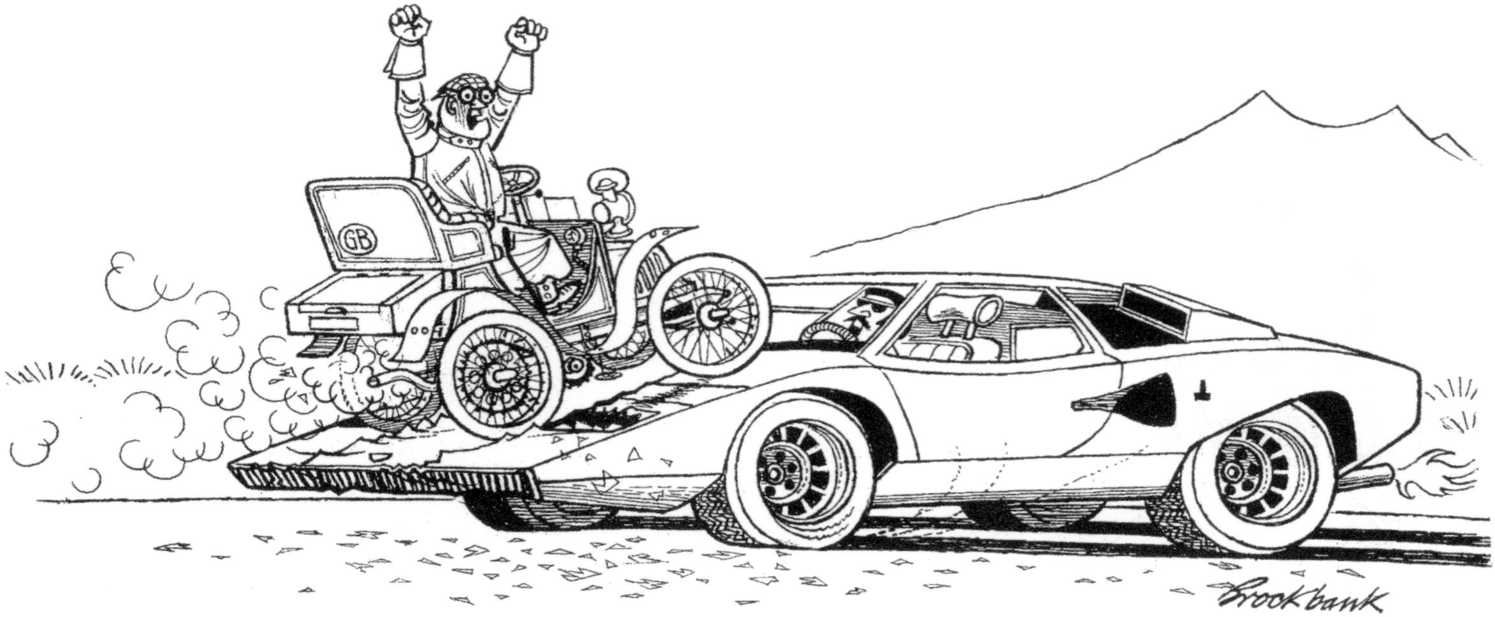
GB
Brockbank

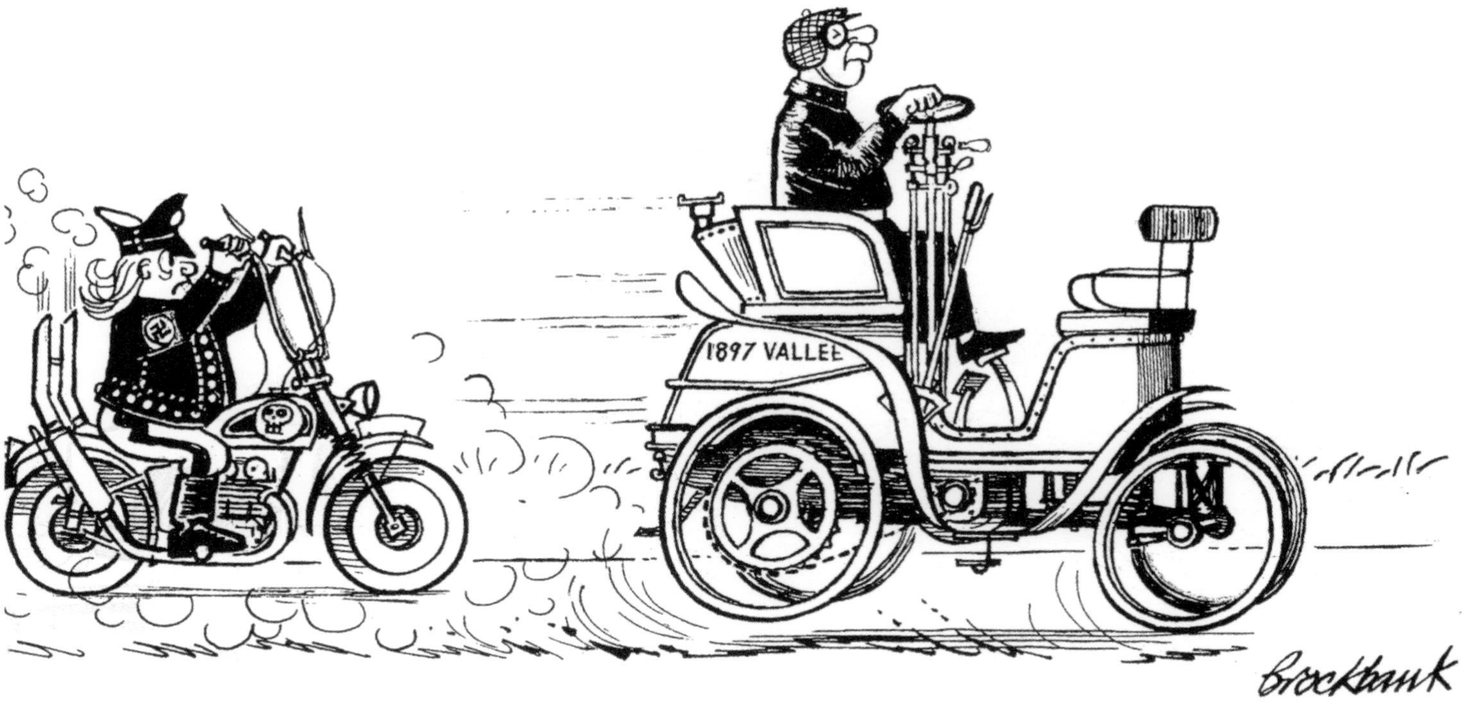
1897 VALLEE
Brockbank

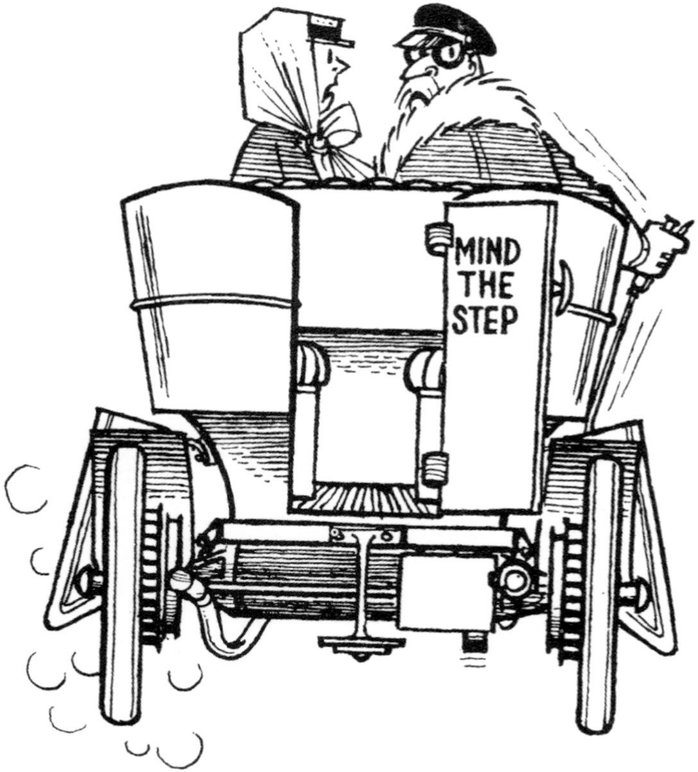
MIND
THE
STEP

'Where's Granny gone?'

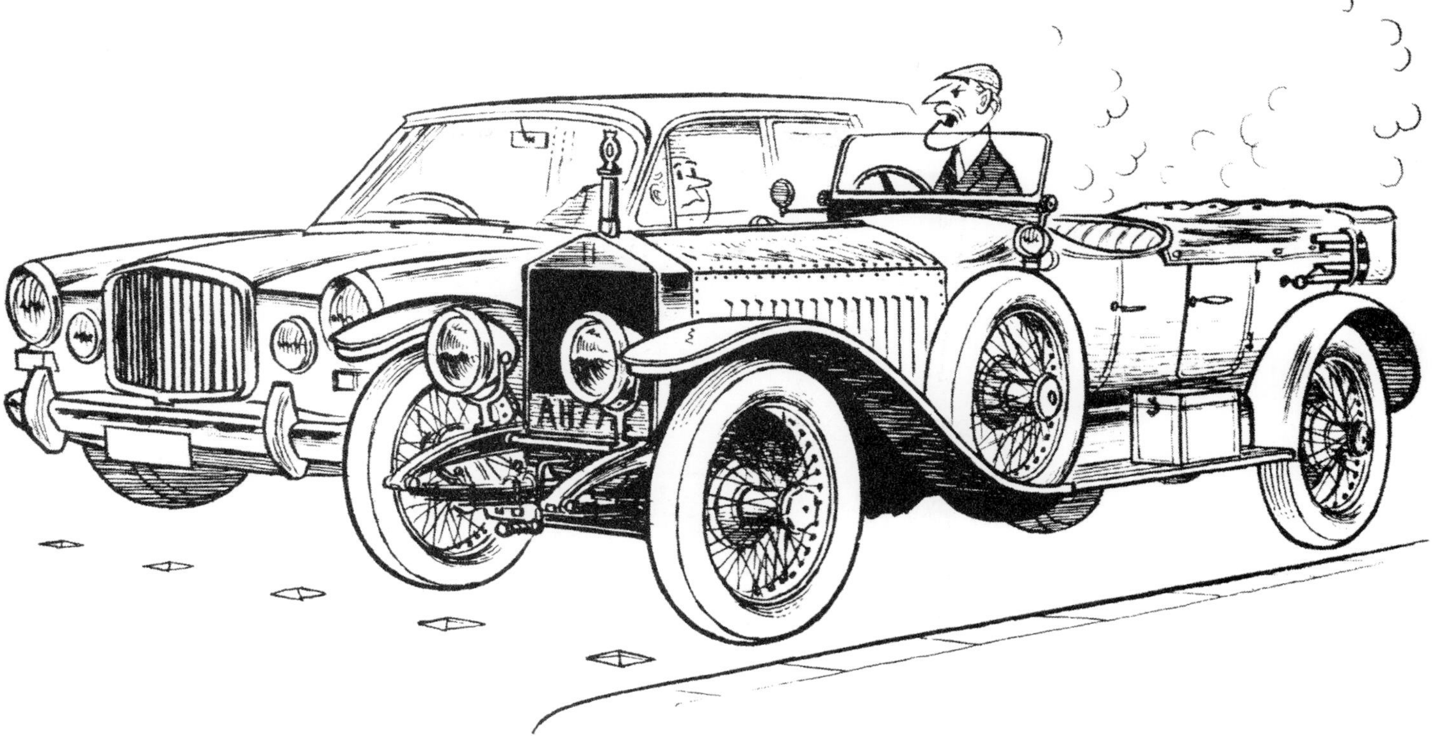

'Distantly related at most, I'd say.'

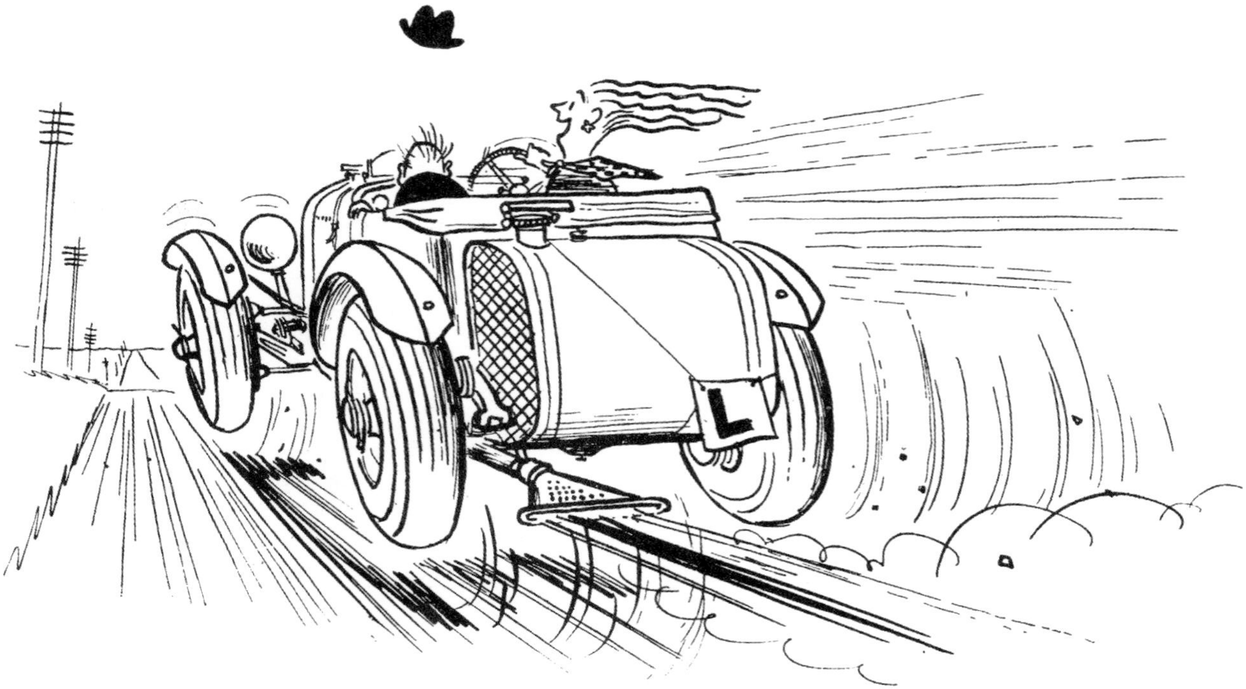
L

‘I call it jolly neighbourly of you, Mr. Fosdyke, to give me the benefit of your 30 years’ experience on the road . . .’

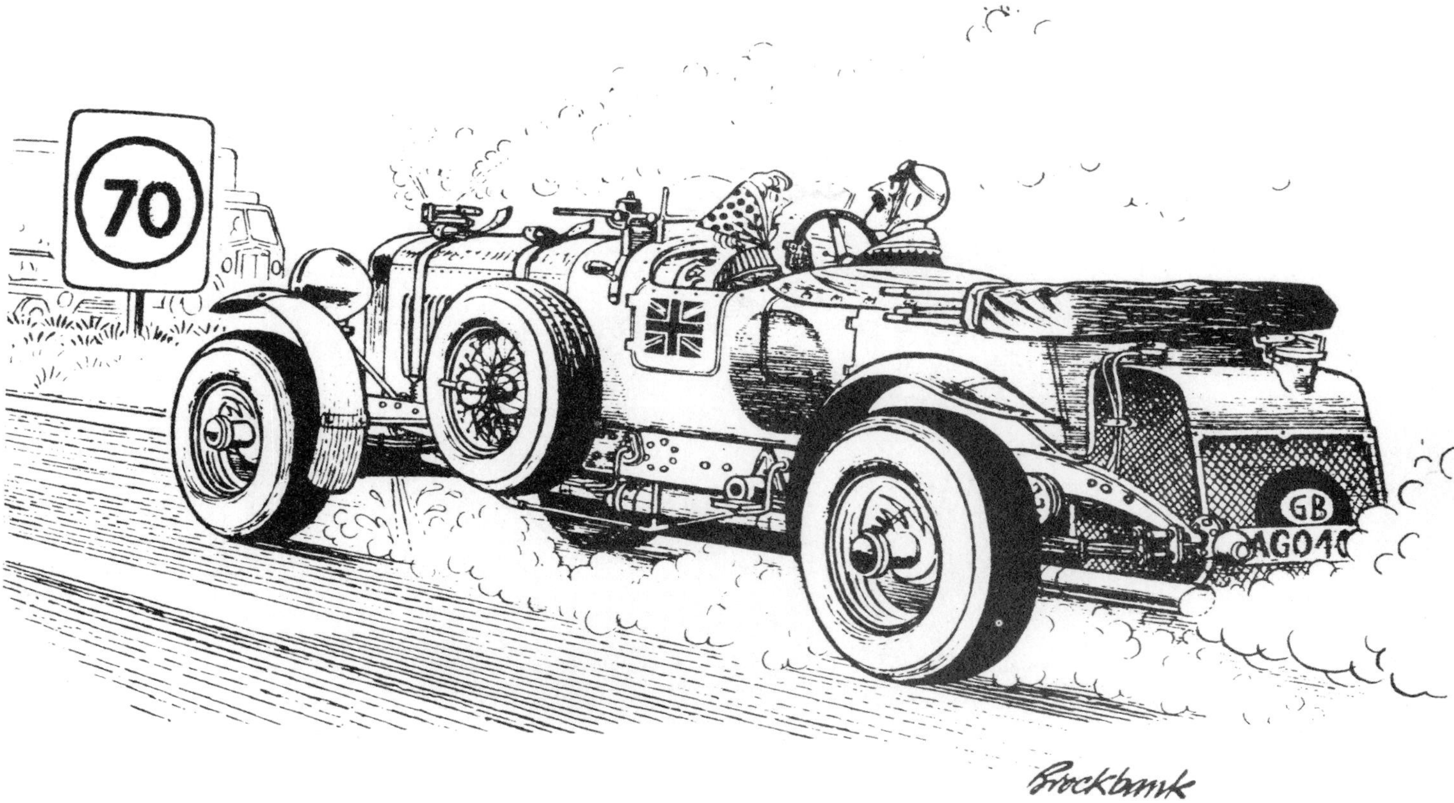
70
GB
AGO40
Brockbank

'I spy with my little eye another fifty quid coming up behind.'

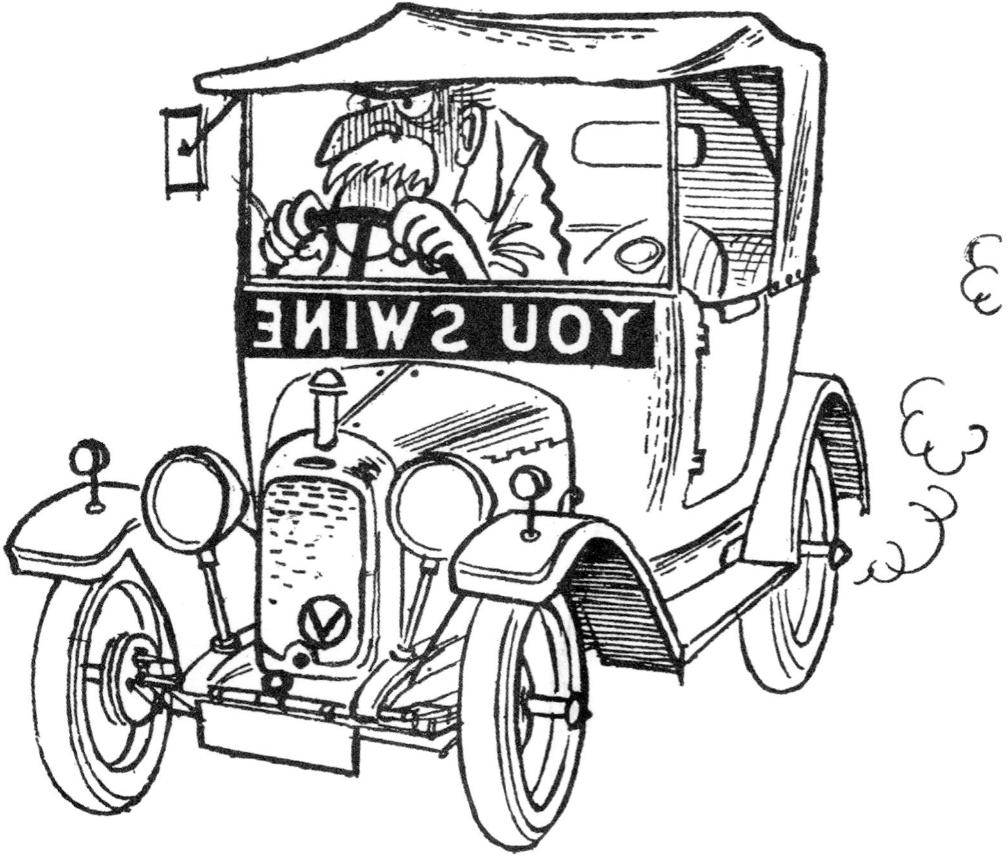
YOU SWINE

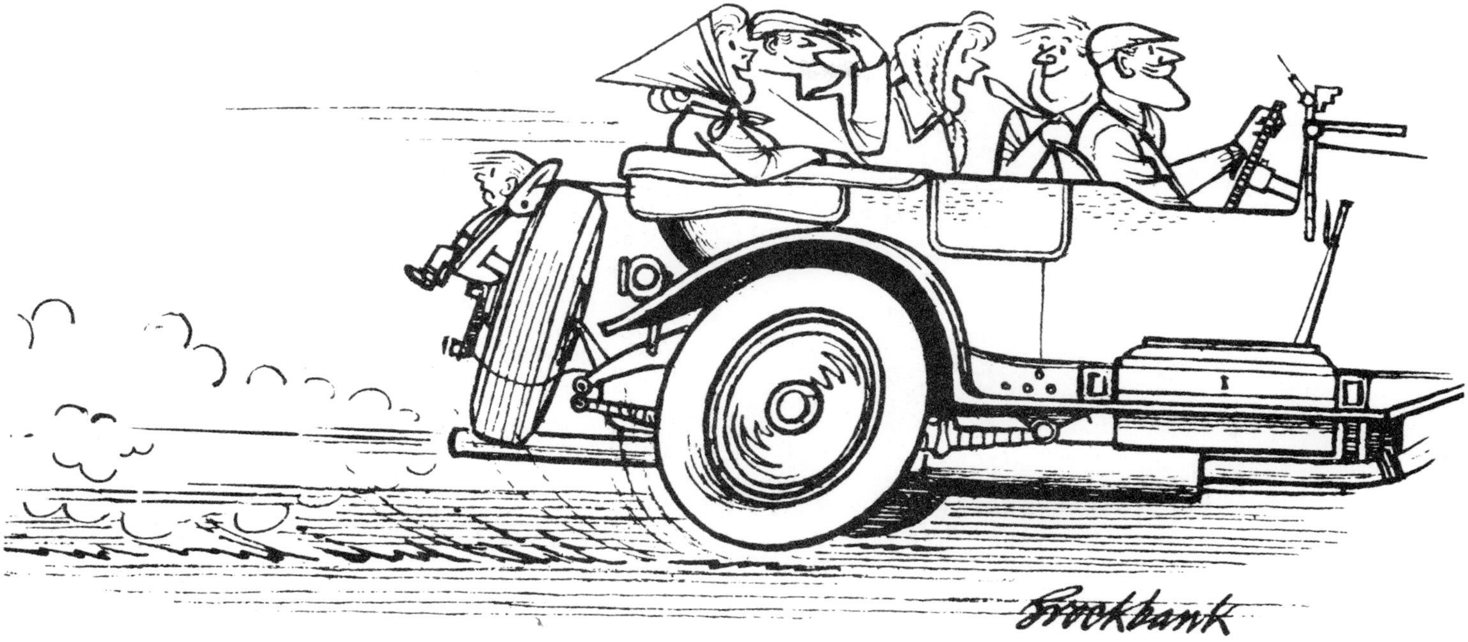
Brockbank

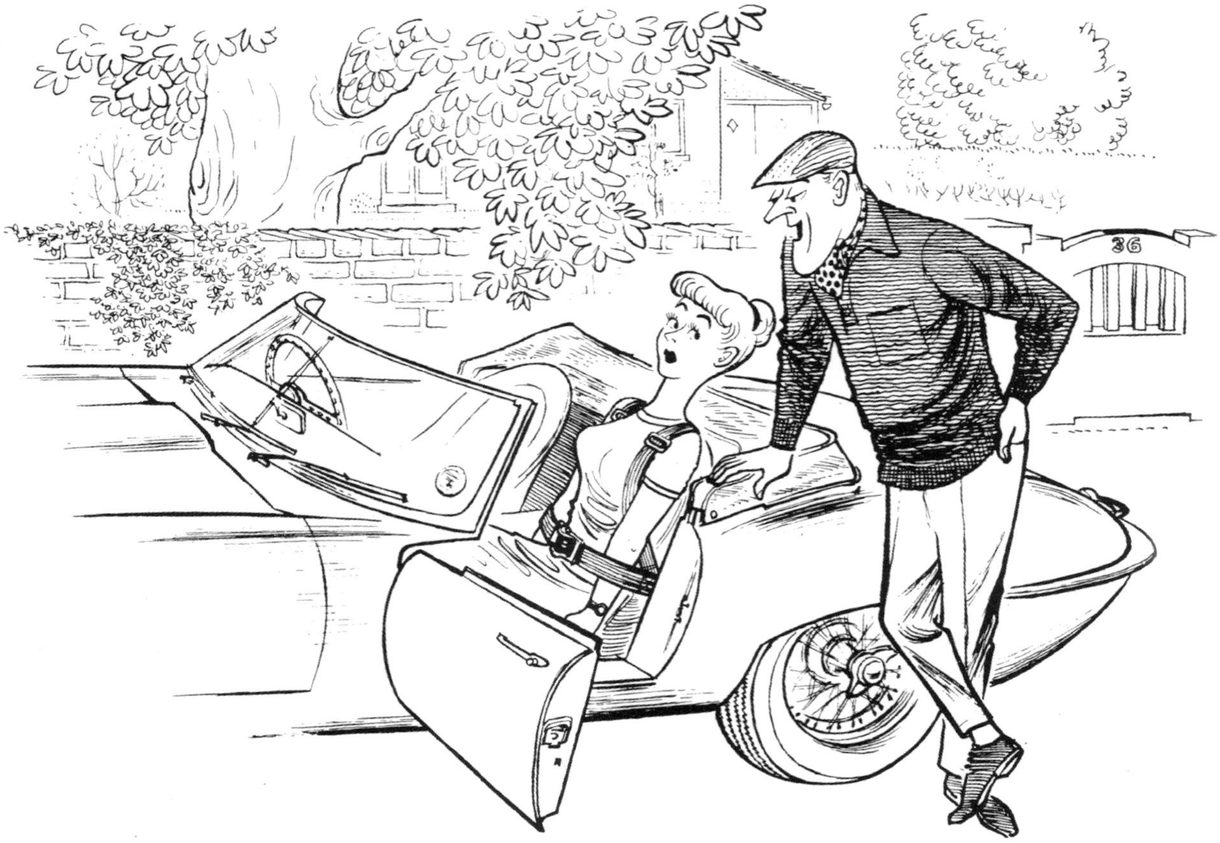
36

'It *is* a bit strange at first, Miss Fitch, but I'm sure the Minister of Transport knows what he's doing.'

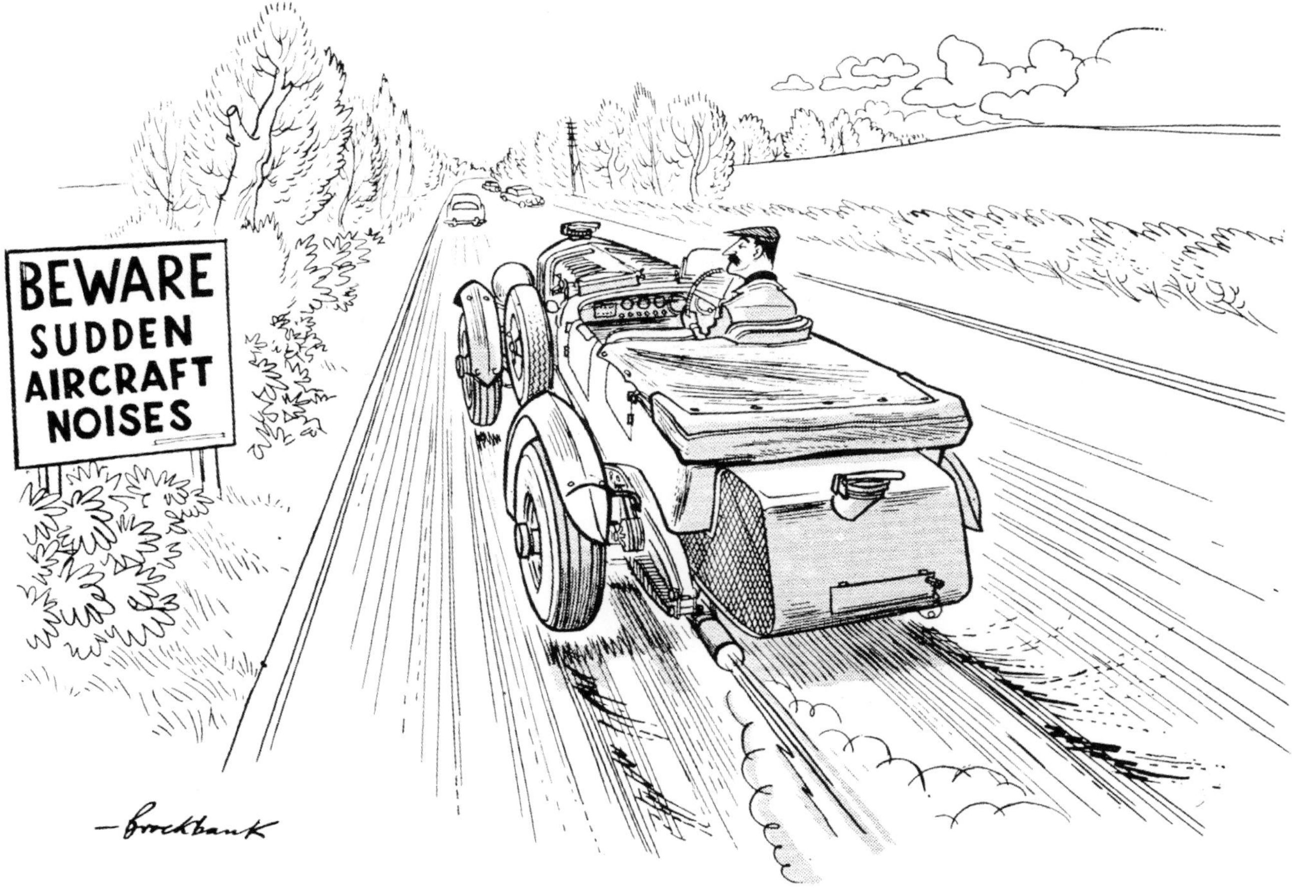
BEWARE
SUDDEN
AIRCRAFT
NOISES
—Brockbank

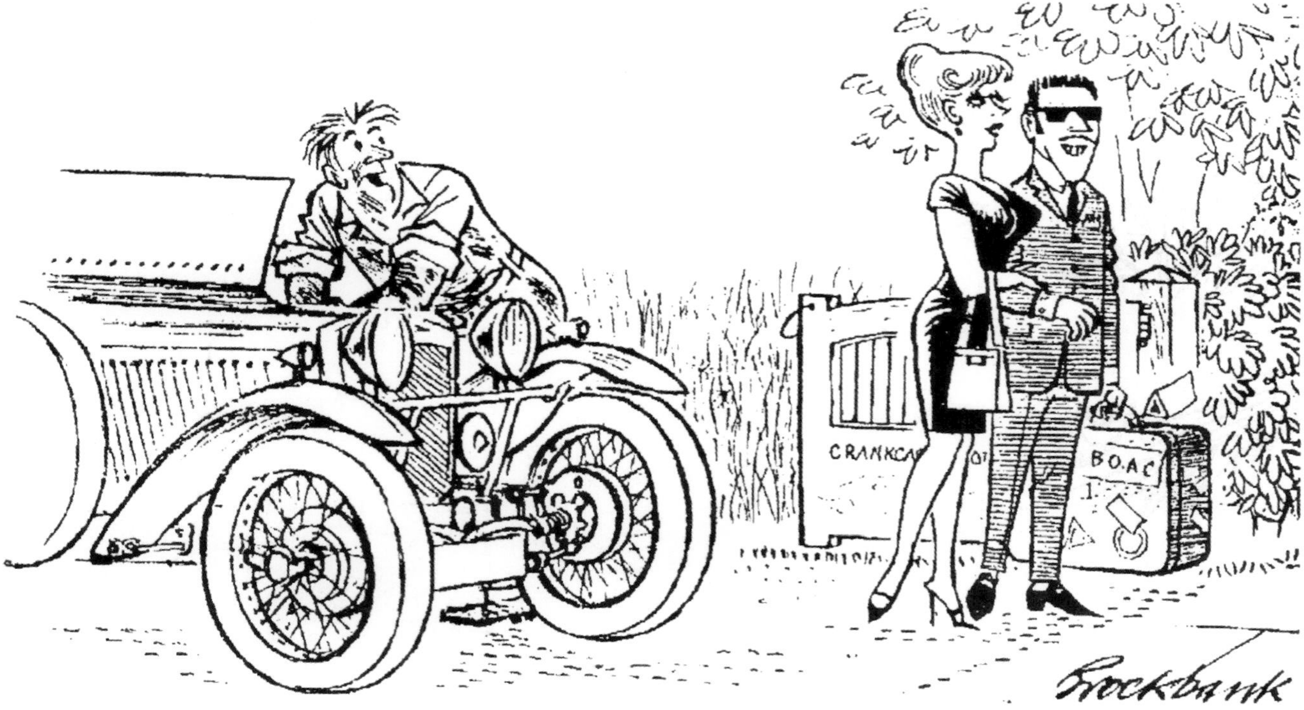
CRANKCA
B.O.AC
Brockbank

'Have a lovely time, dear, and you too, Angelo.'

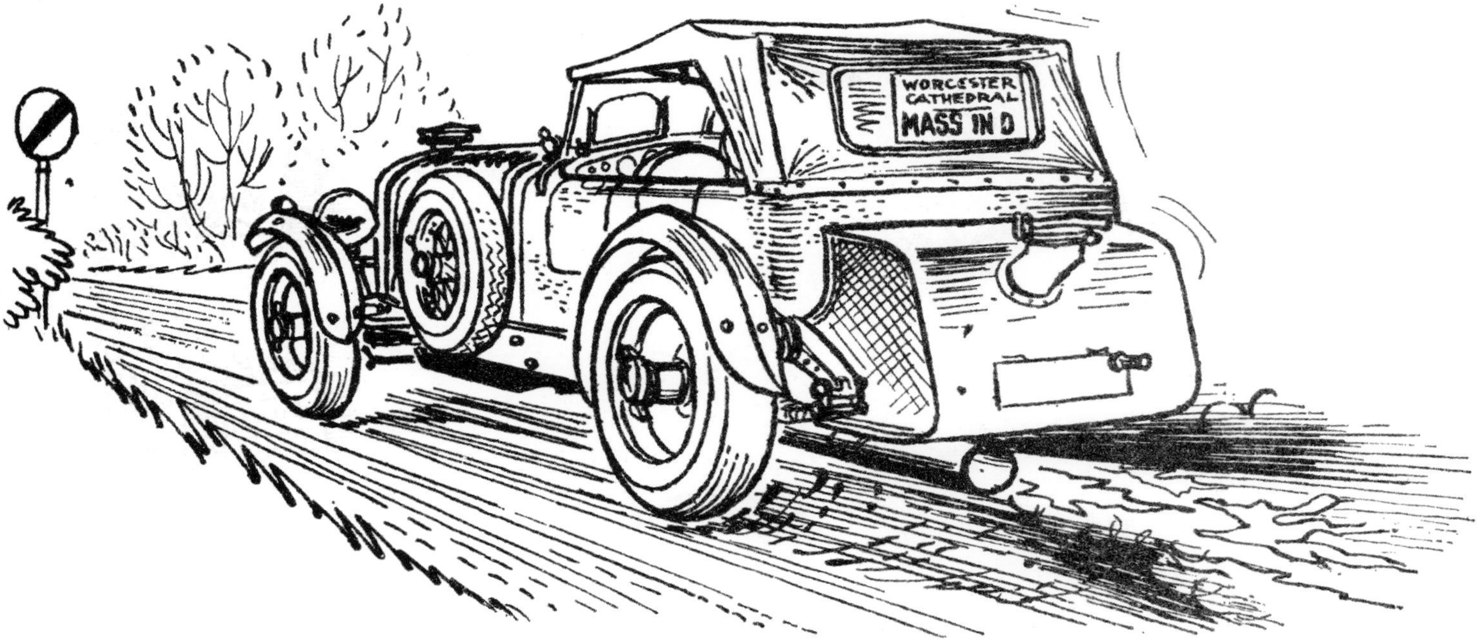
WORCESTER CATHEDRAL
MASS IN D

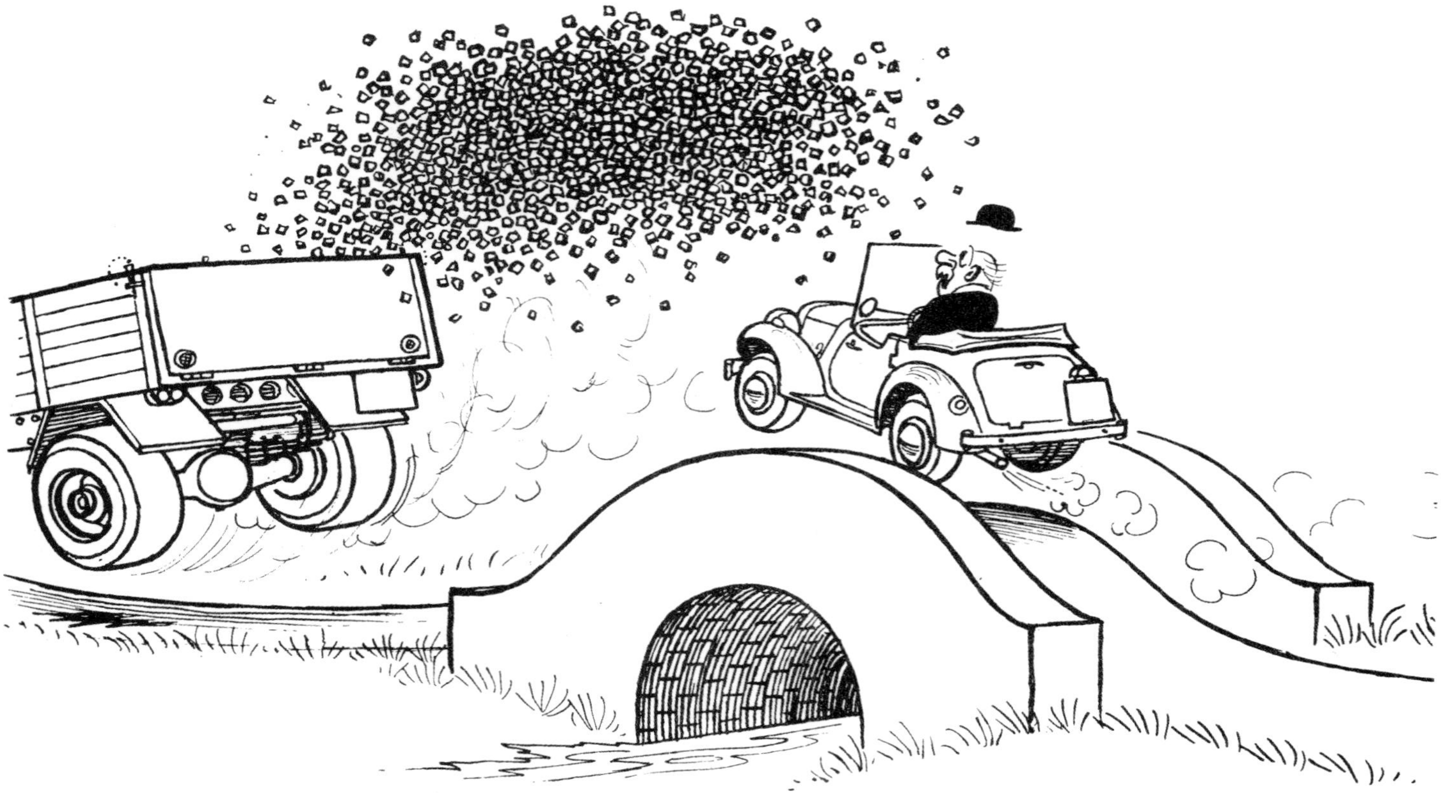

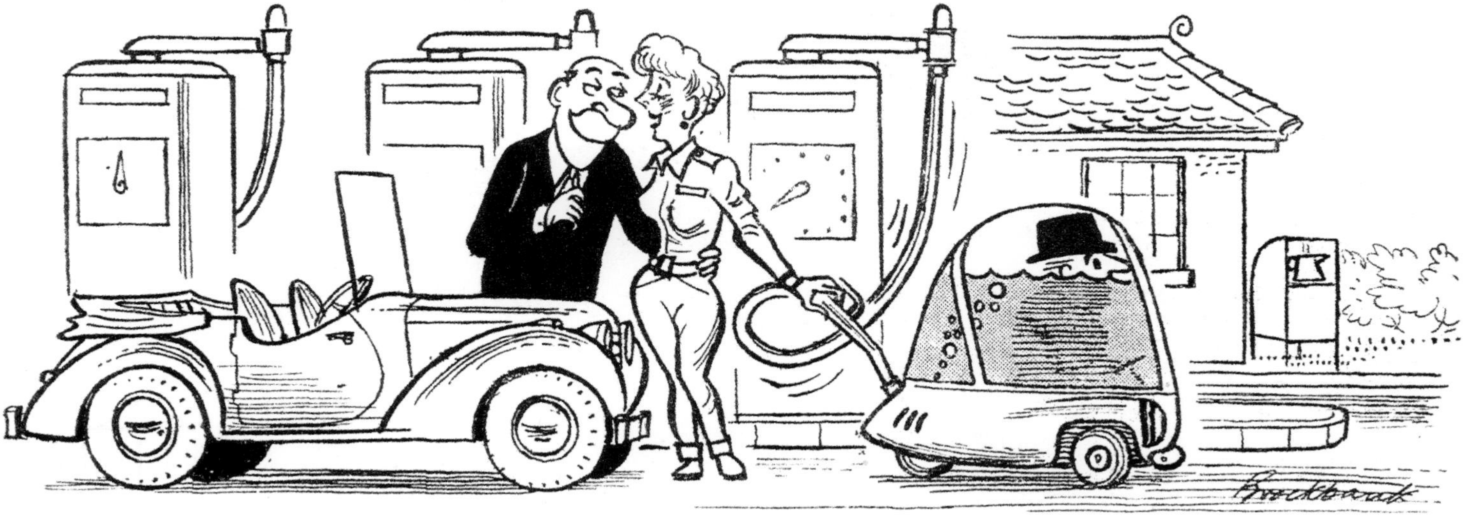
Brockbank

Brockbank

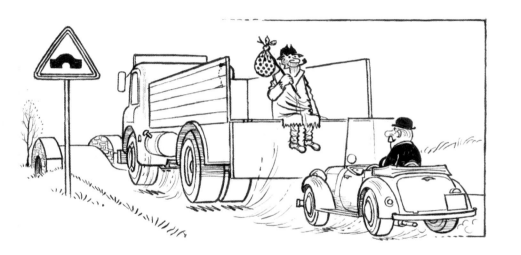

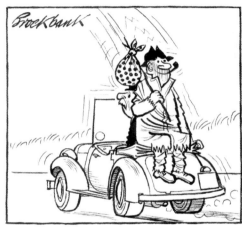

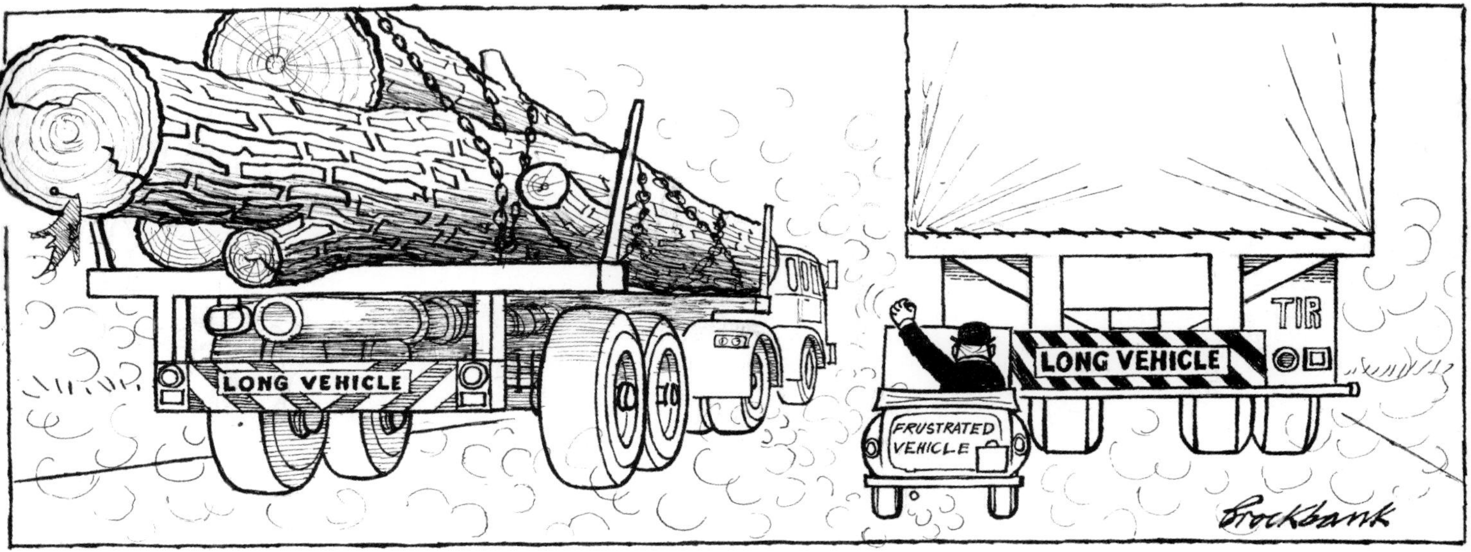
LONG VEHICLE
FRUSTRATED VEHICLE
TIR
LONG VEHICLE
Brockbank

RB.

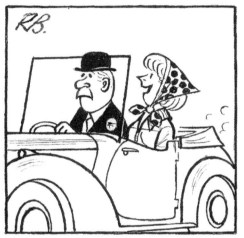

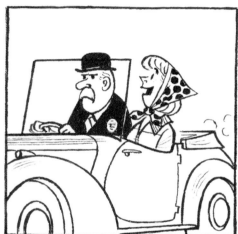

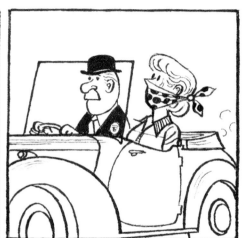

Brockbank

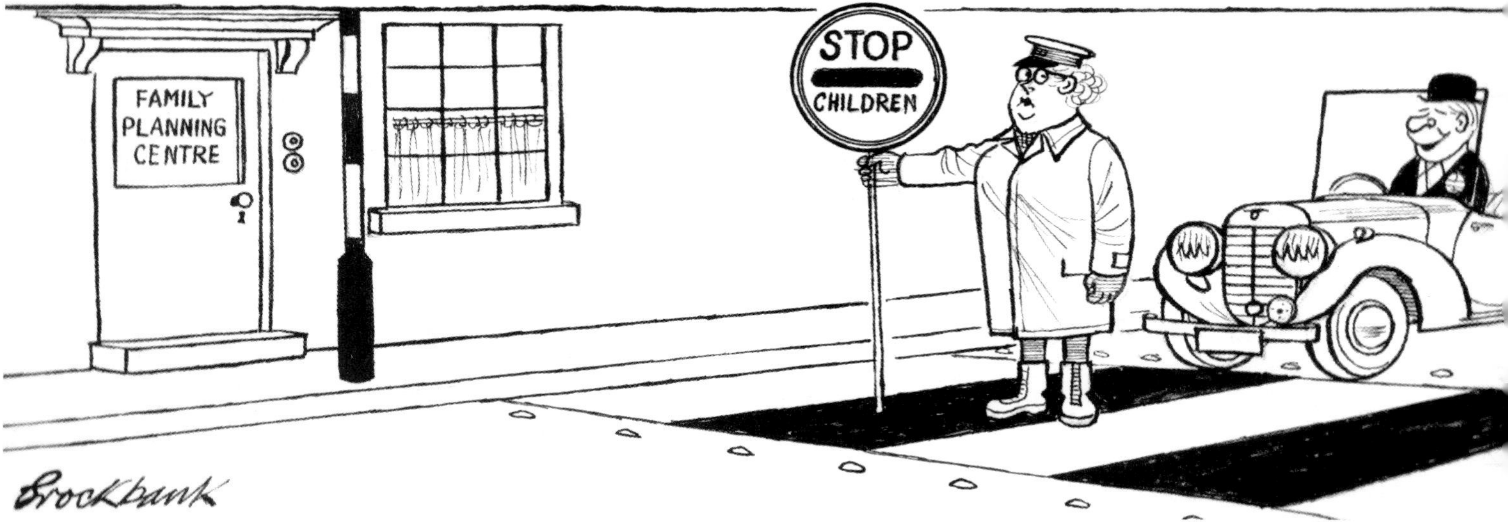
FAMILY
PLANNING
CENTRE
STOP
CHILDREN
Brockbank

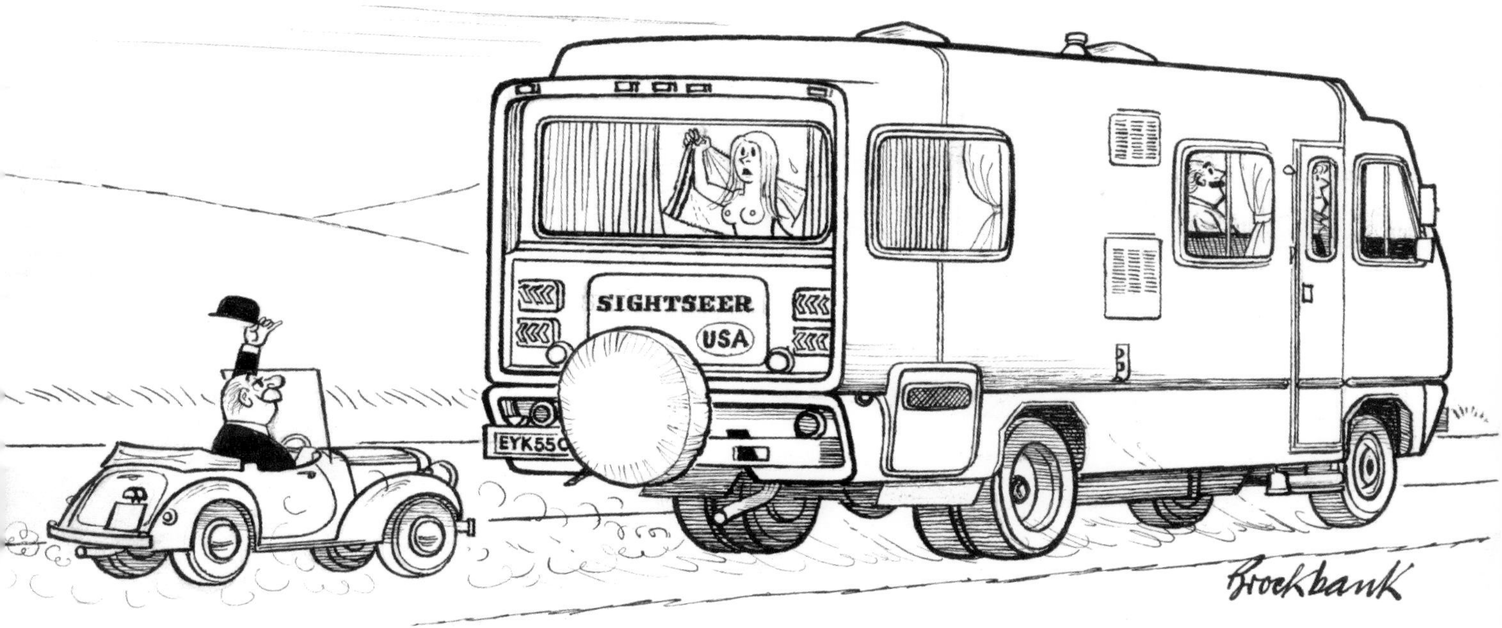
SIGHTSEER
USA
EYK55C
Brockbank

Brockbank

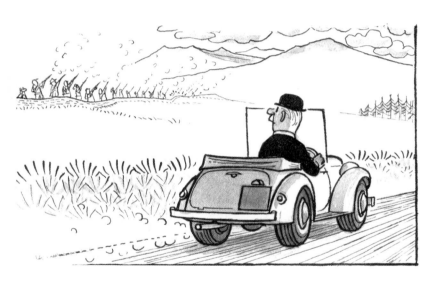

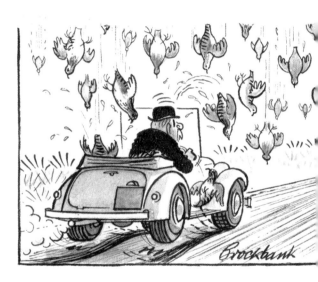

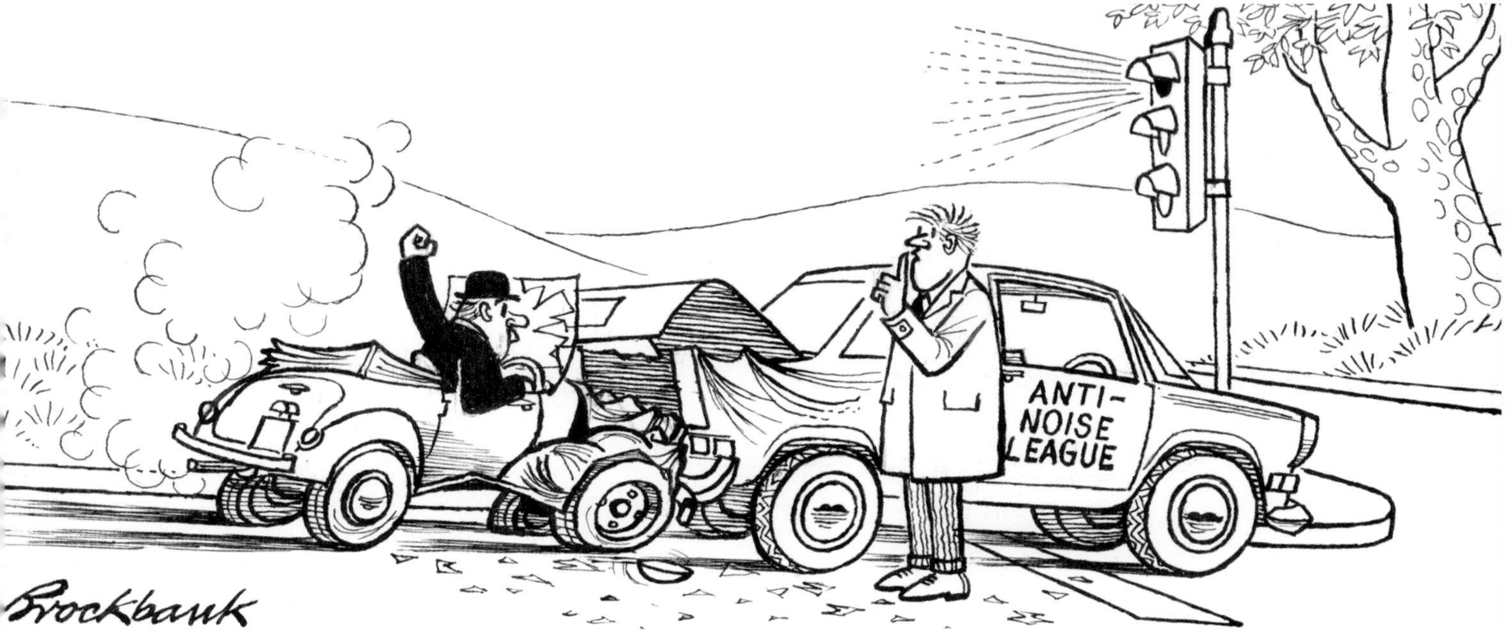
ANTI-
NOISE
LEAGUE
Brockbank

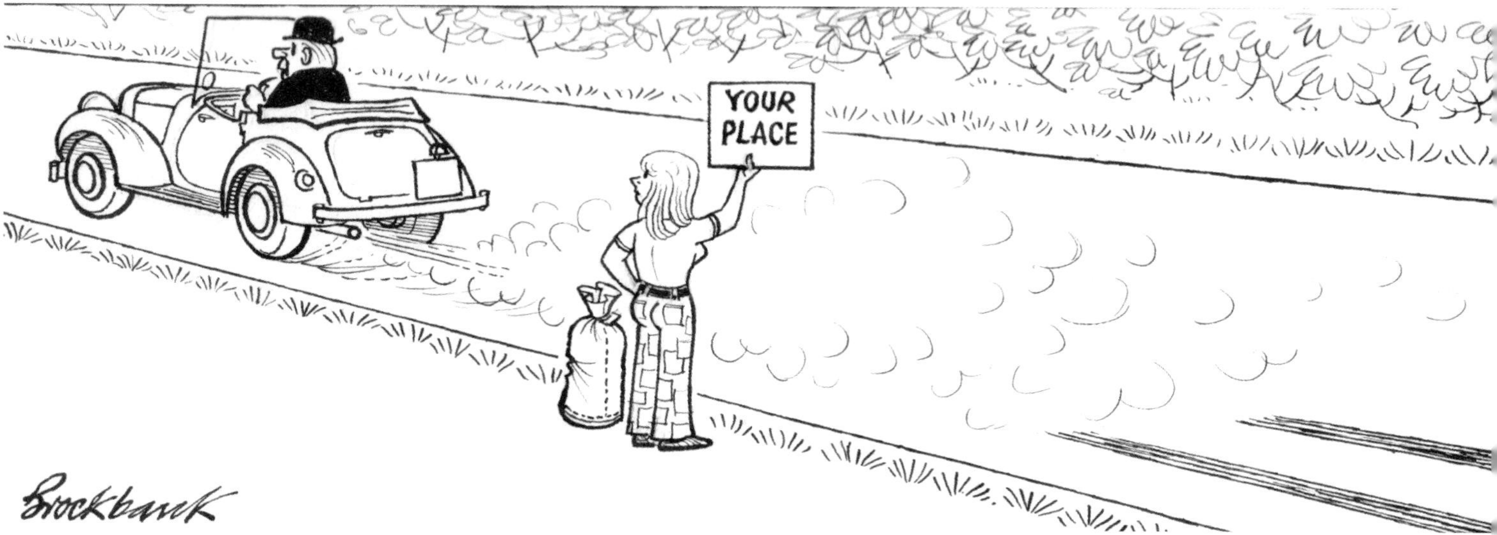
YOUR PLACE
Brockbank

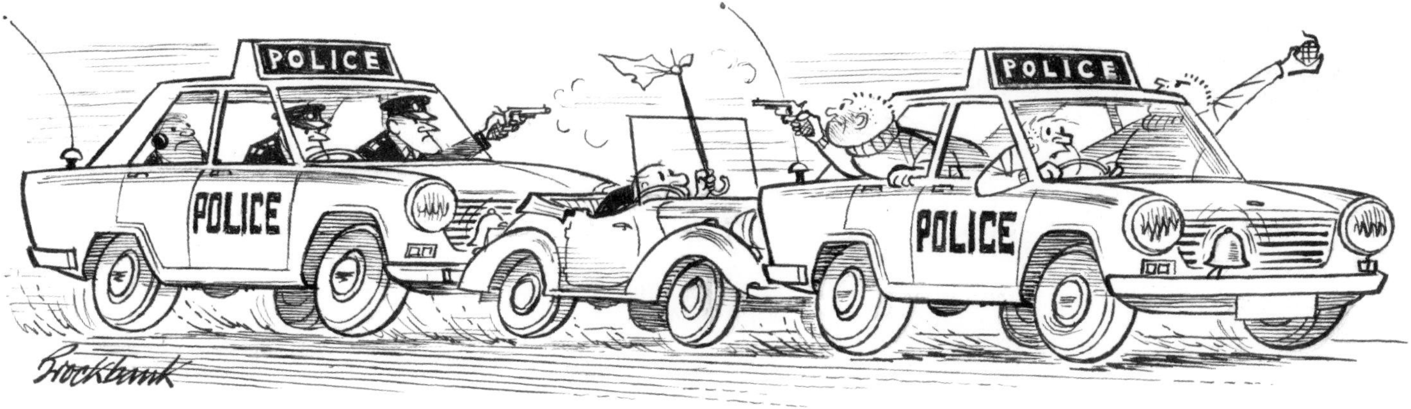
POLICE
POLICE
POLICE
POLICE
Brockbank

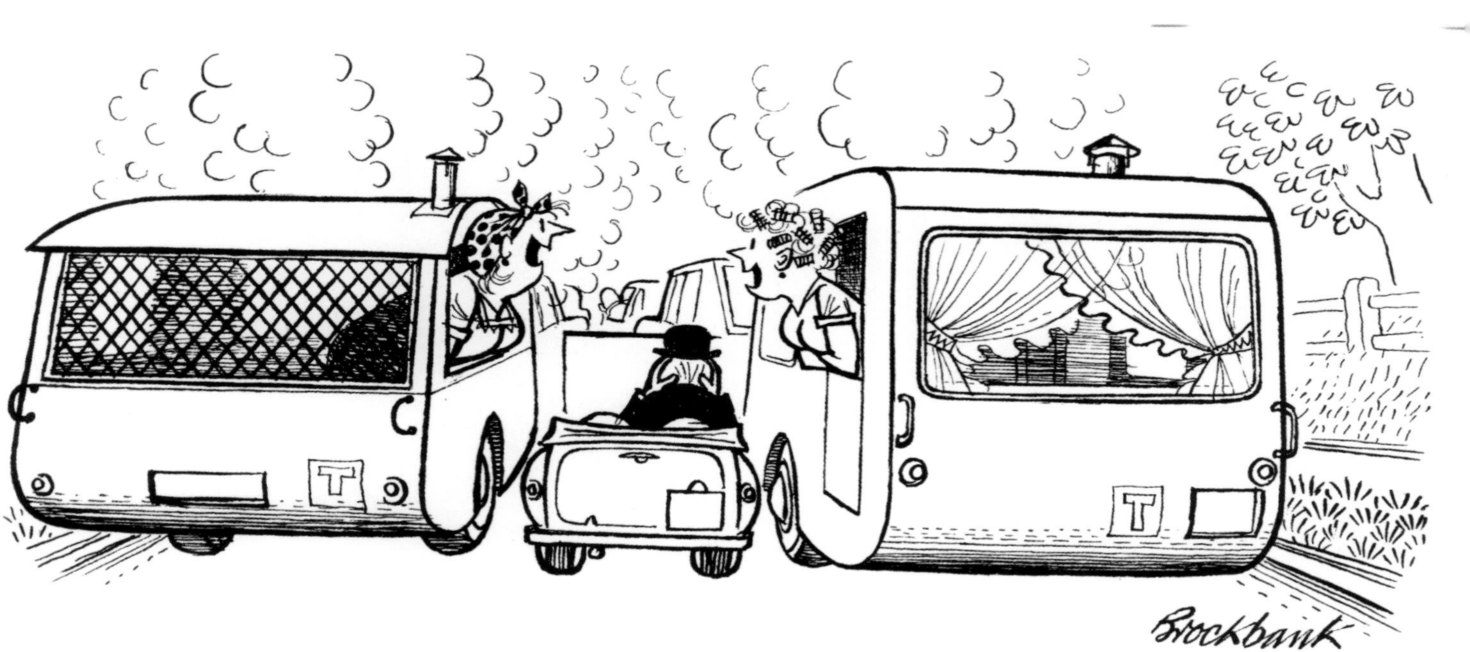
Brockbank

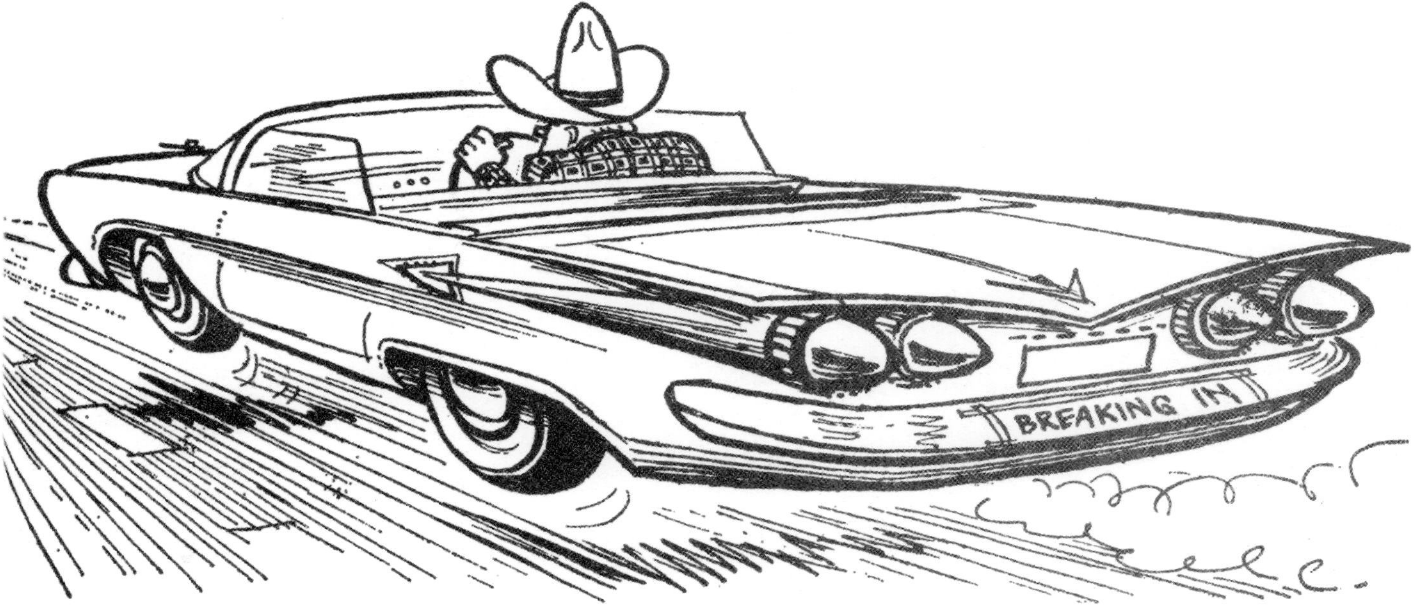
BREAKING IN

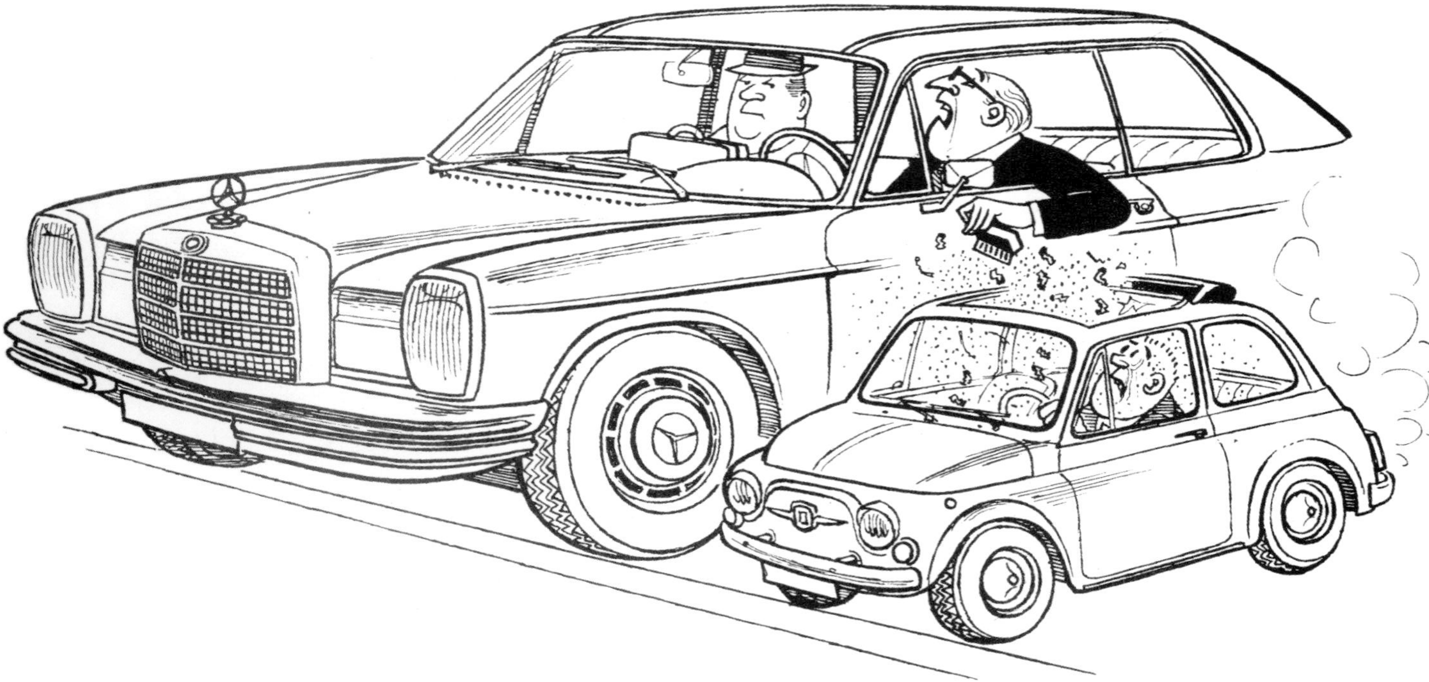

‘Being affluent enough to possess such a splendid car hasn’t in the least altered my attitude to the lower orders’

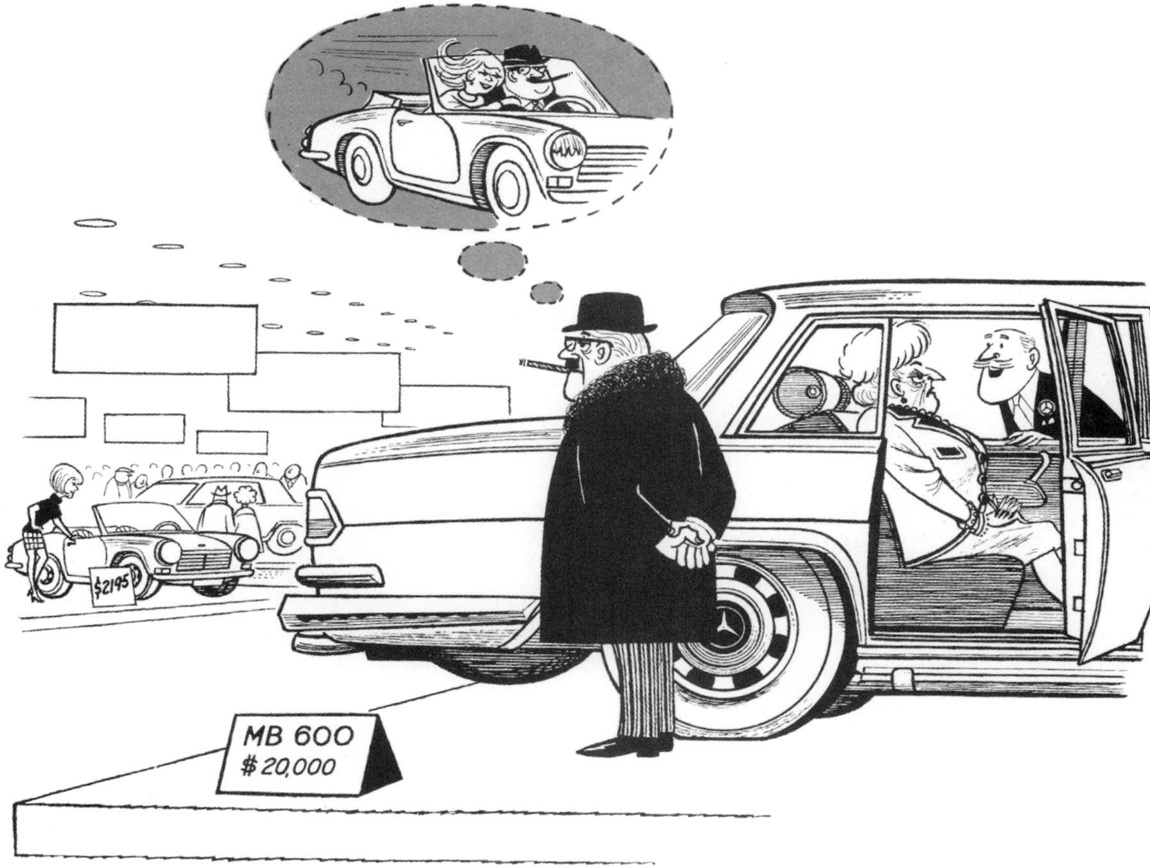
$2195
MB 600
$ 20,000

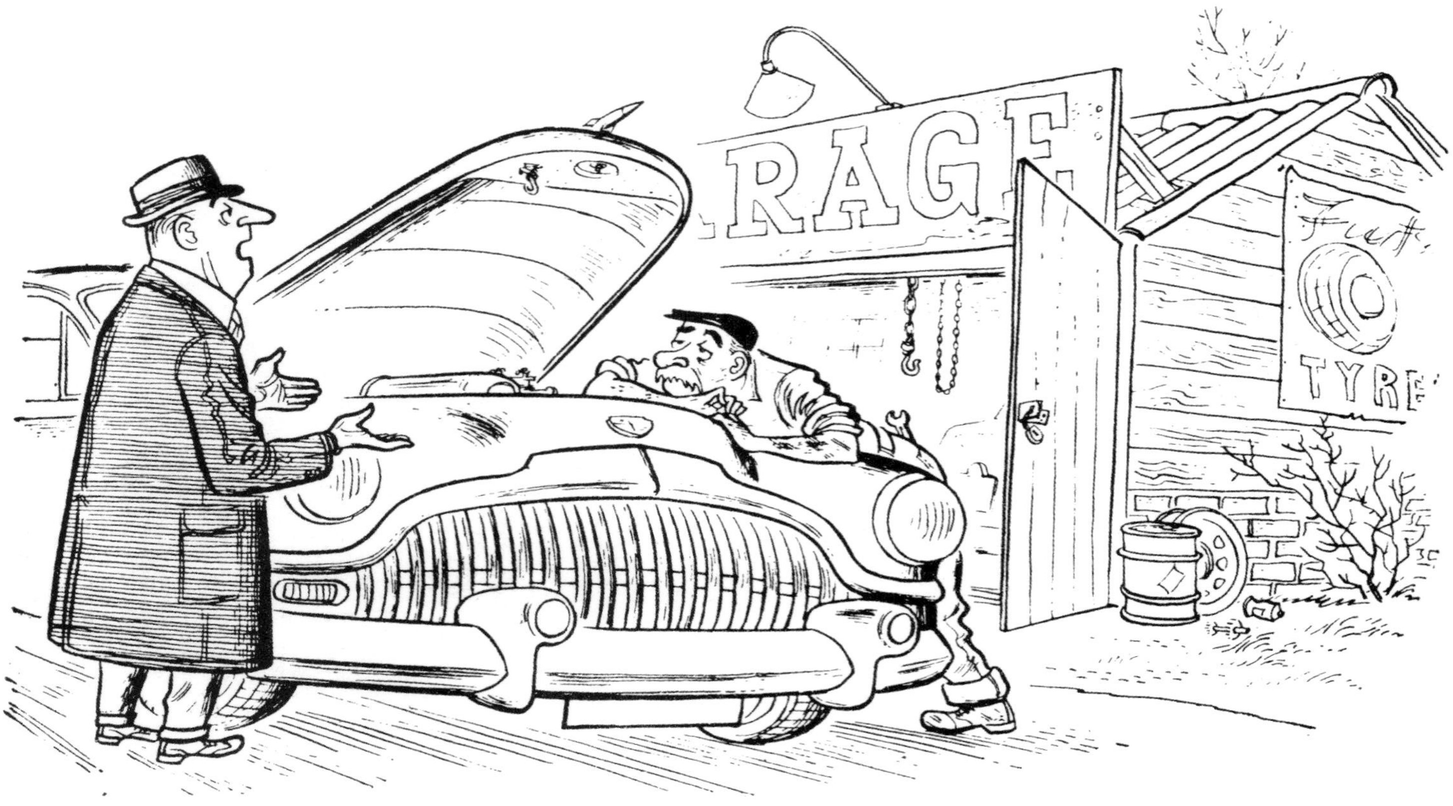
RAGE

‘I’ve checked the Dynasurge Drive, the Gas Miser and the Hydromatic Sweetsurger, and I’m *still* short of Fireball Power.’

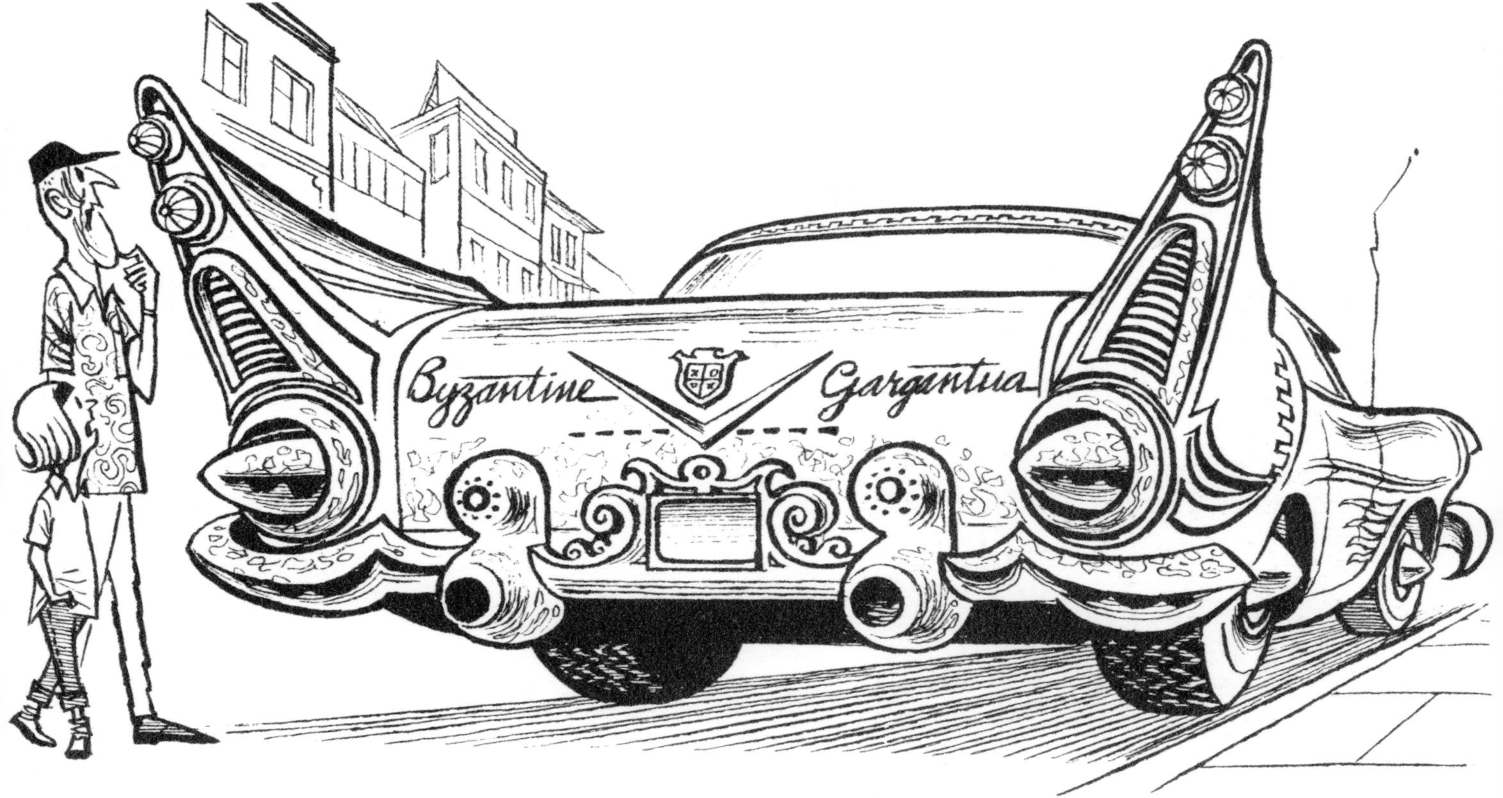

Byzantine
Gargantua

'Do you mean to say you and Mom actually *owned* a thing like *that?*!!'

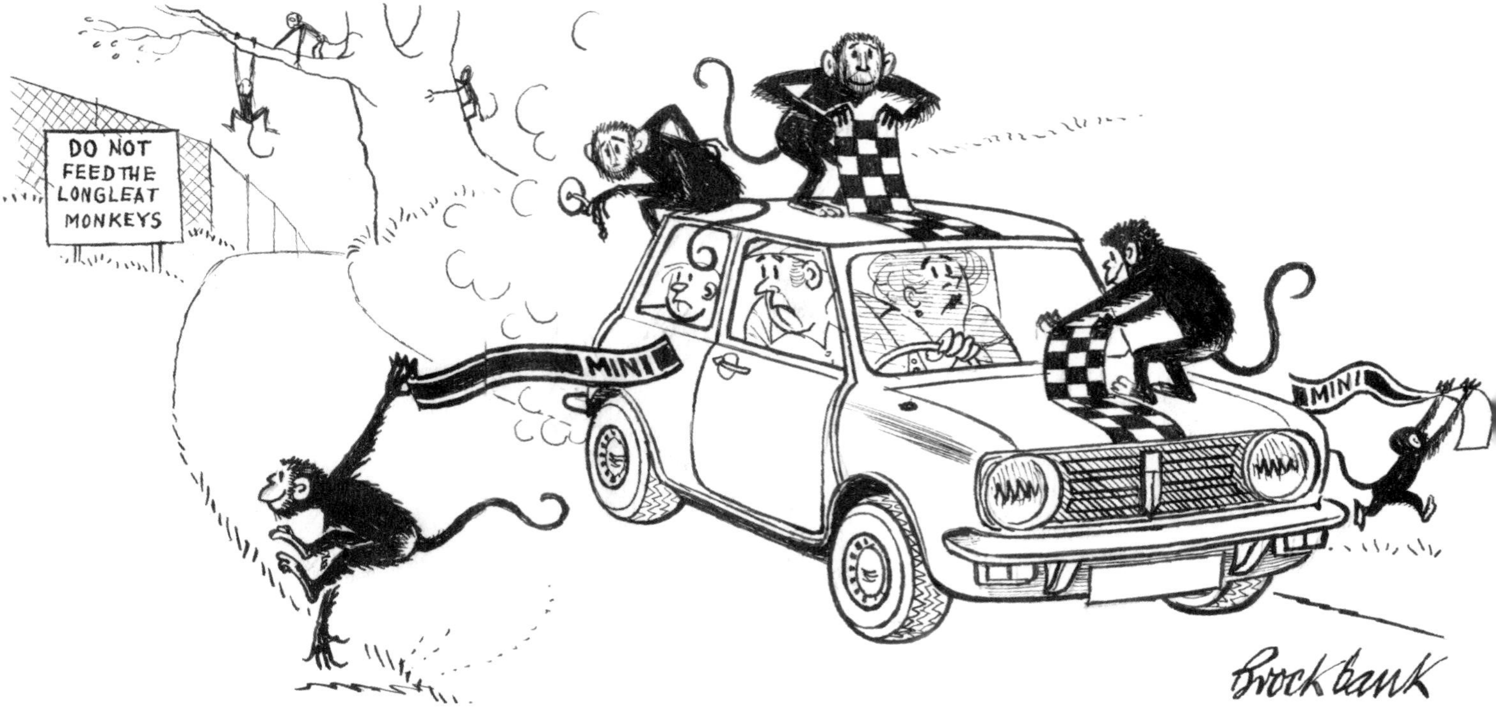
DO NOT FEED THE LONGLEAT MONKEYS
MINI
MINI
Brockbank

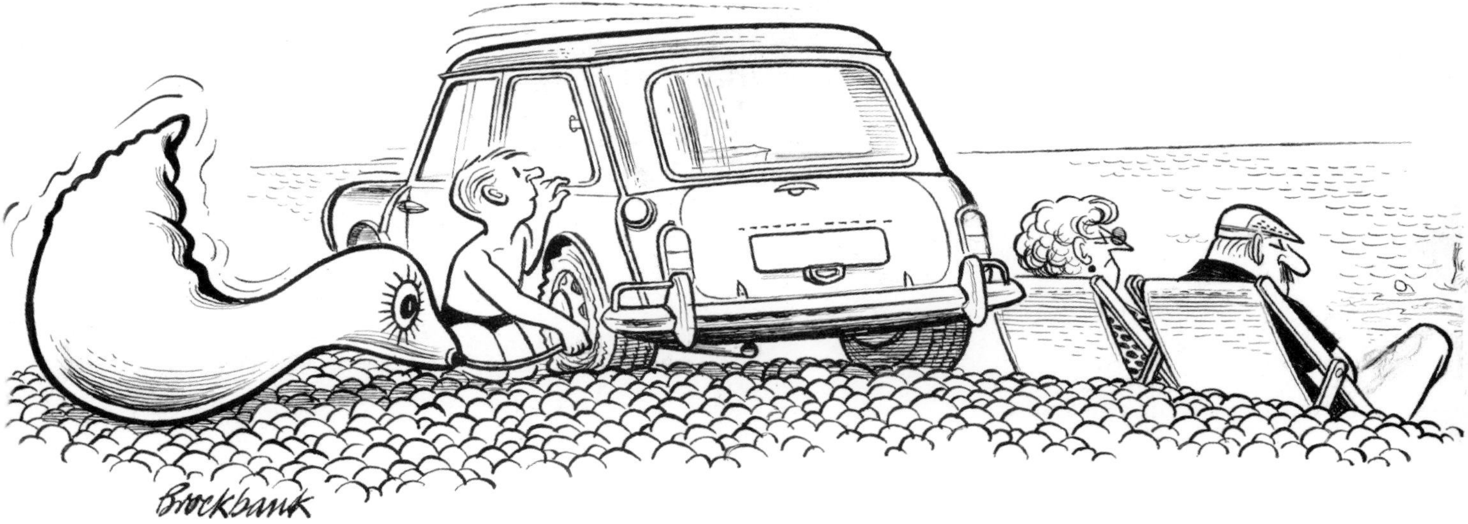
Brockbank

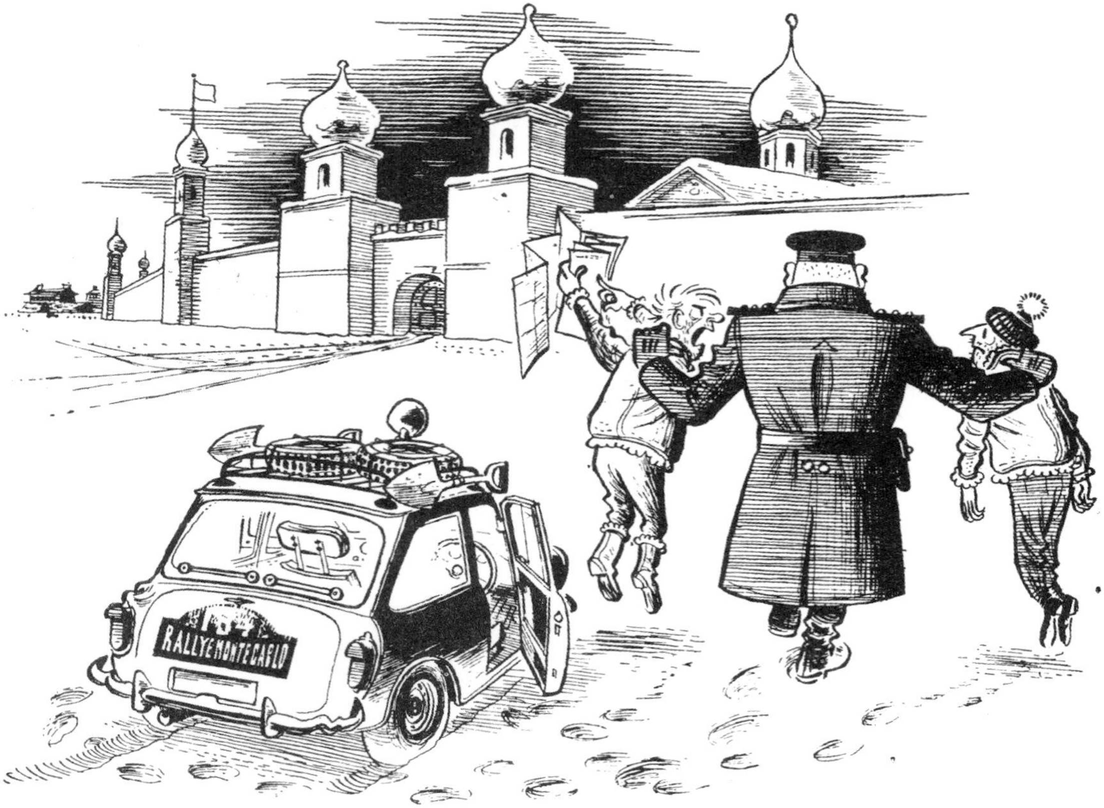
RALLYE MONTE CARLO

'I told you we shouldn't have turned left at Gdynia.'

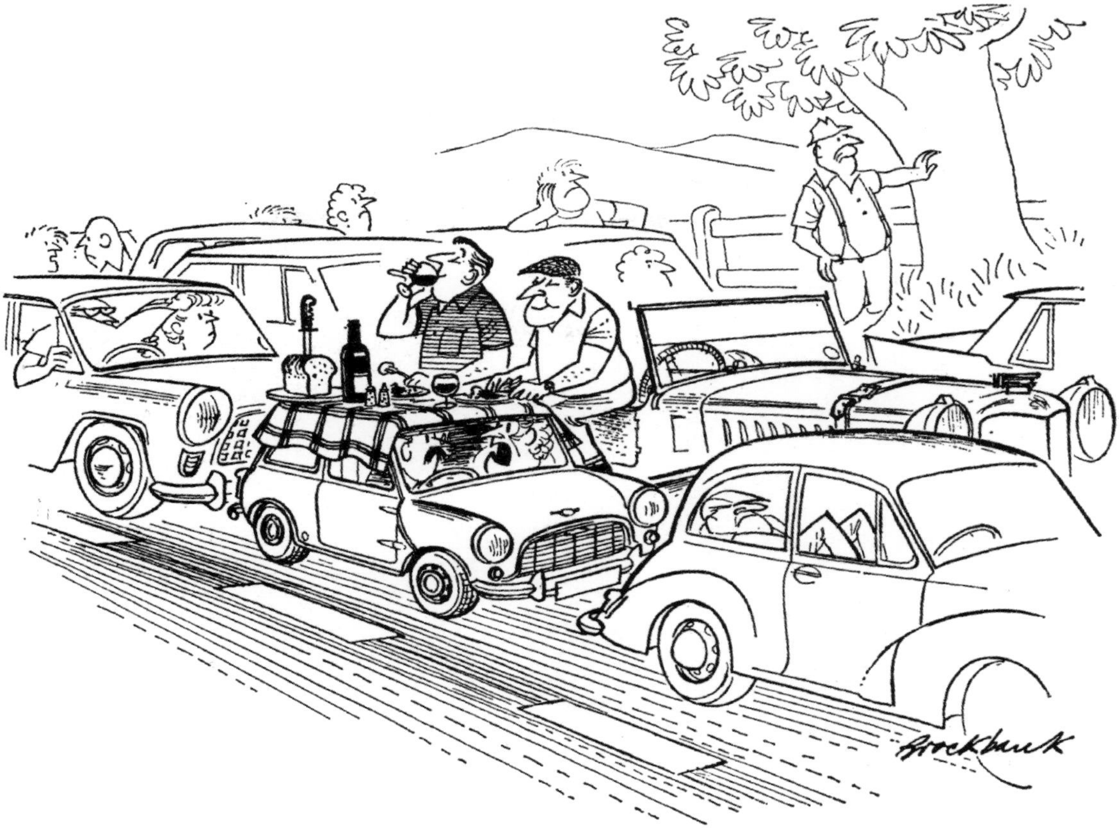

'He must learn to live with Mini-cars as best he can . . .'

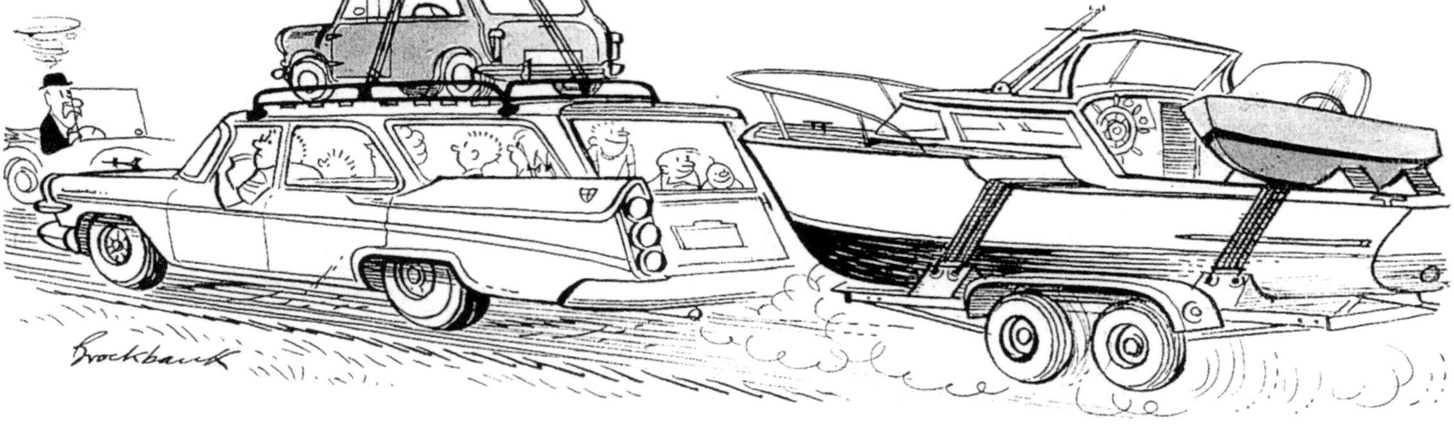
Brockbank

On Holiday with Spares

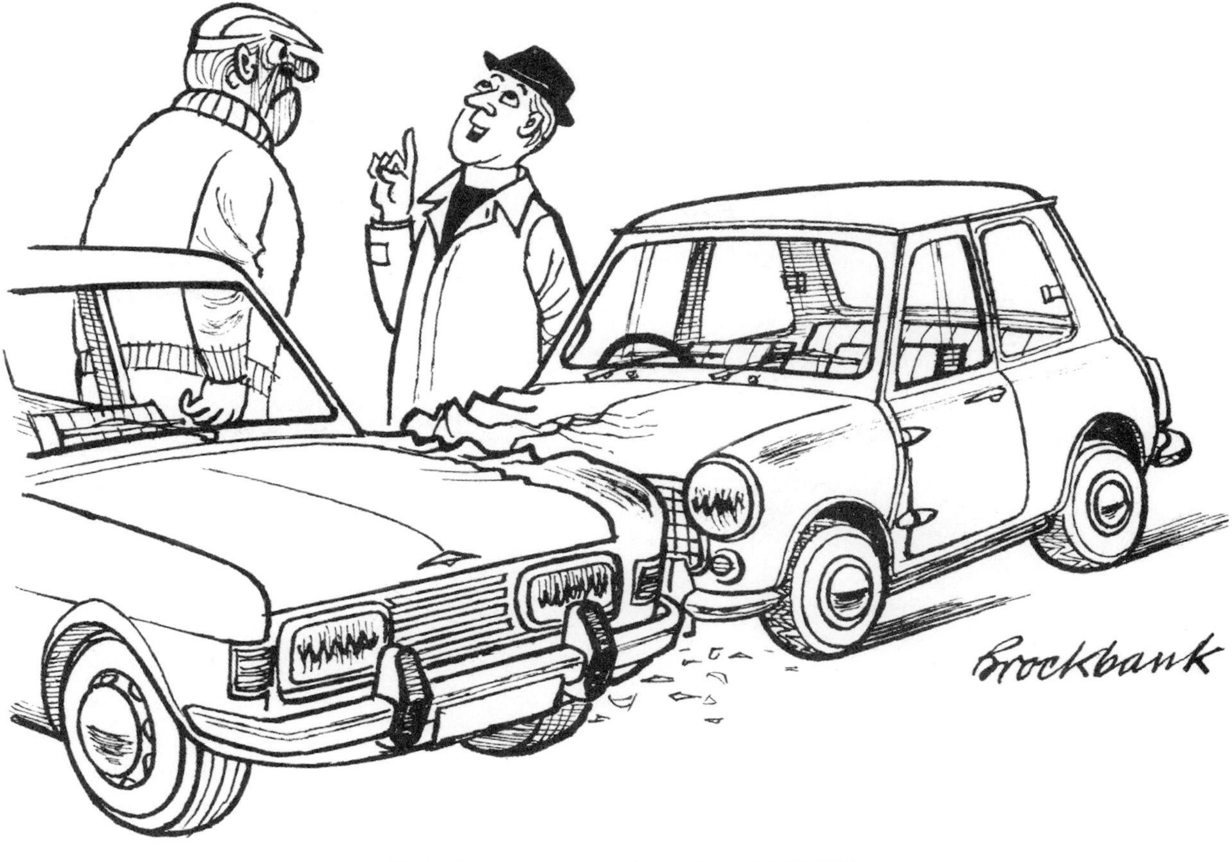
Brockbank

'It is just your word against OURS?'

'Ah, that can only be that beautiful copper-plate handwriting my mother always says belongs to a more gracious, kindly gentlemanly age.'

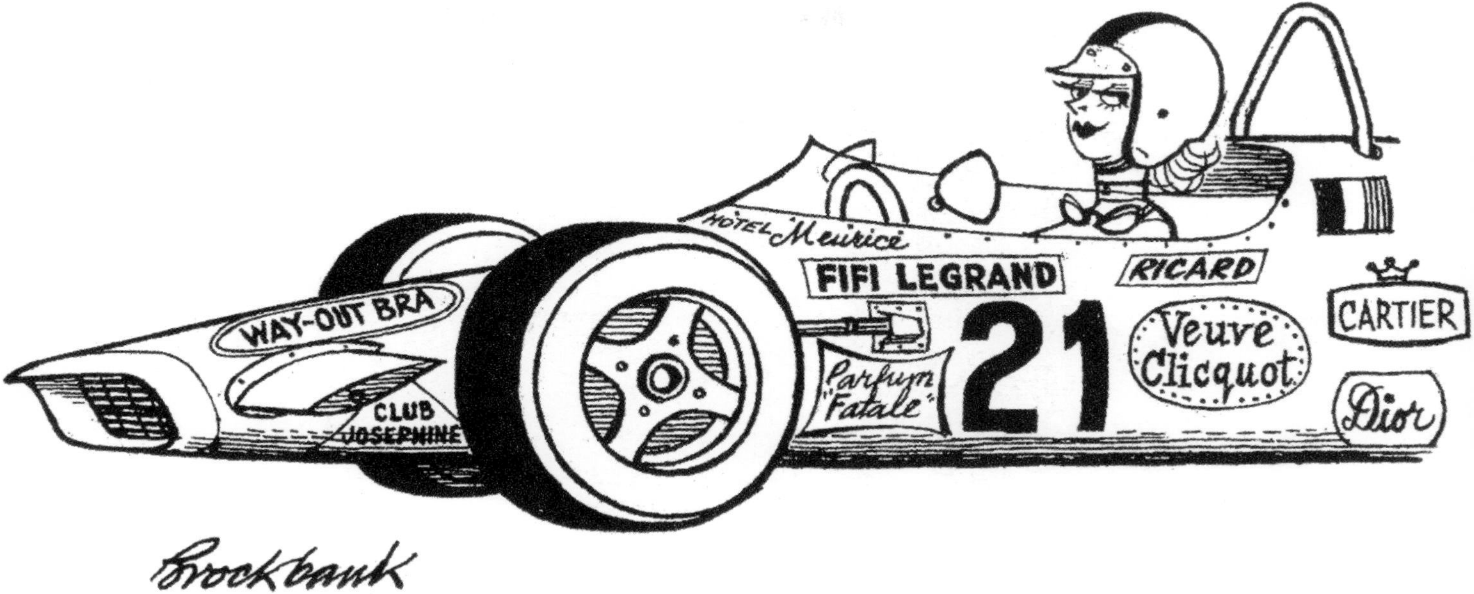
HOTEL Meurice
FIFI LEGRAND
RICARD
WAY-OUT BRA
CLUB JOSEPHINE
21
Parfum "Fatale"
Veuve Clicquot
CARTIER
Dior
Brockbank

Fifi le Grand

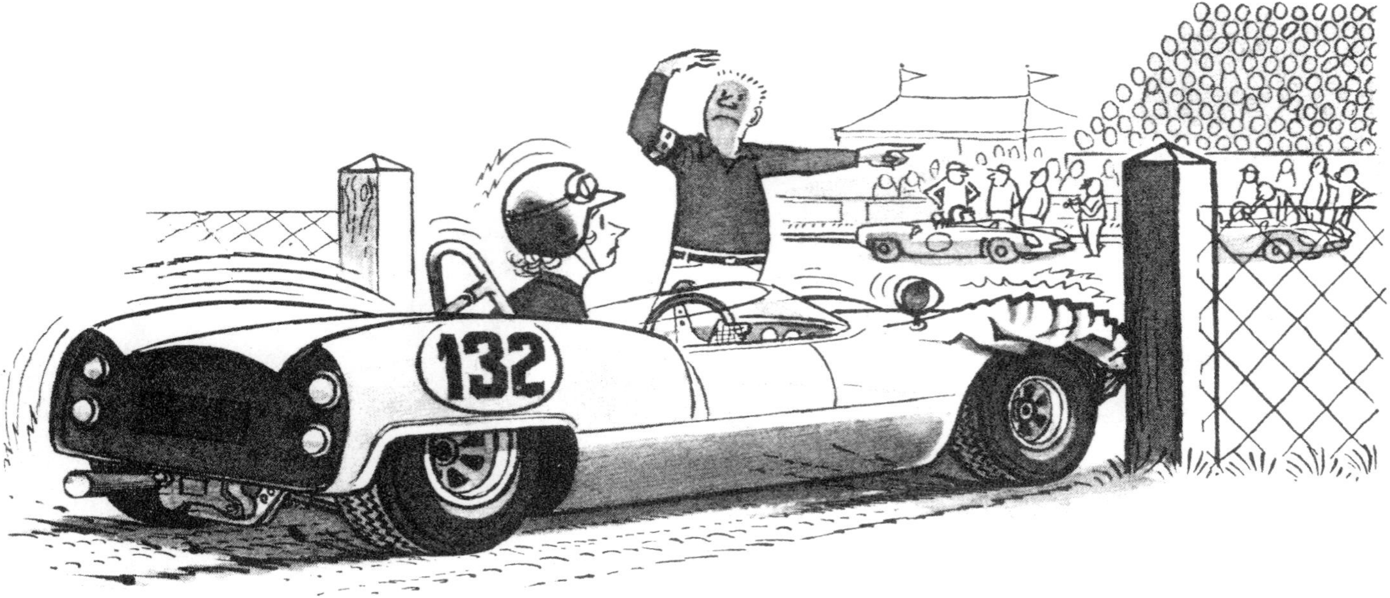
132

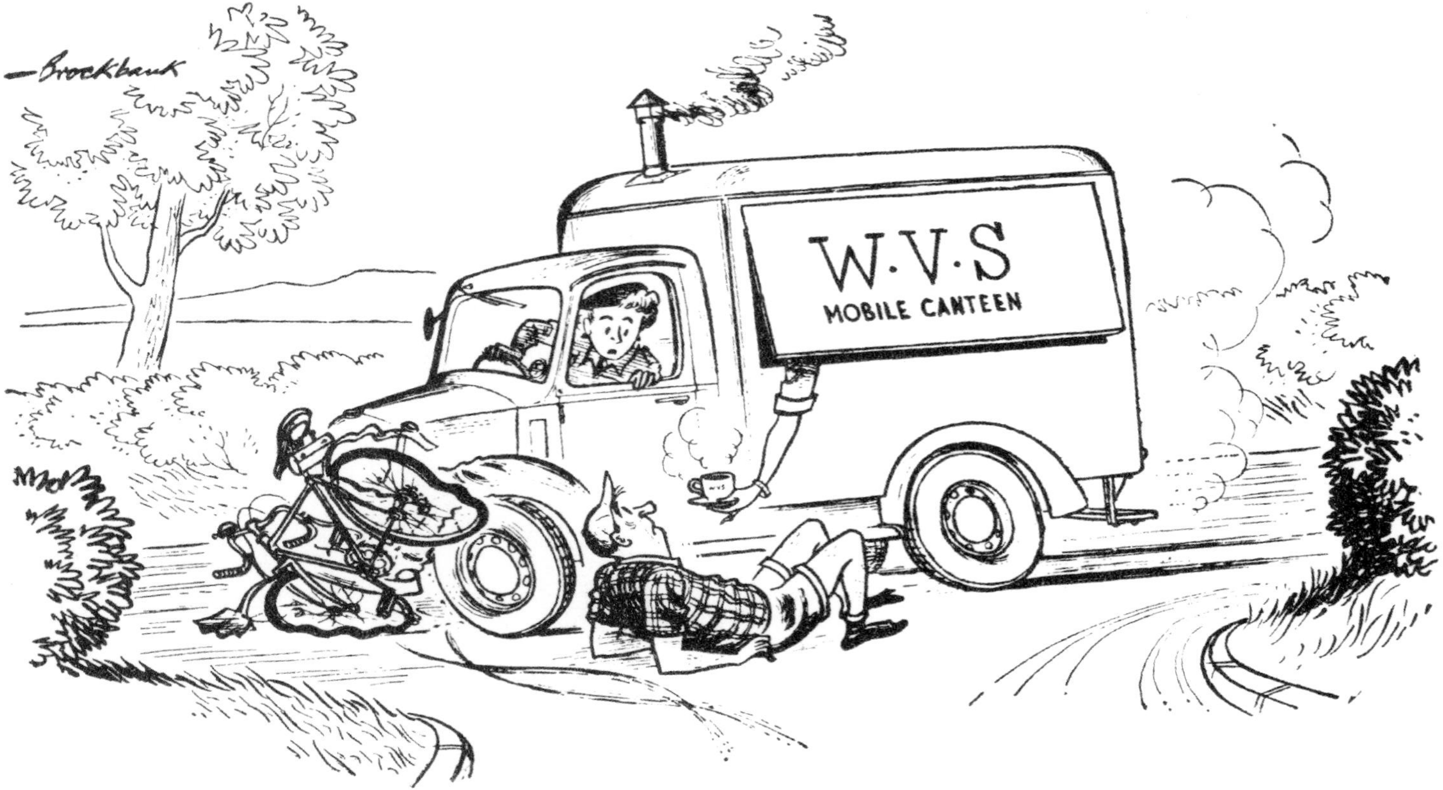
—Brockbank
W·V·S
MOBILE CANTEEN

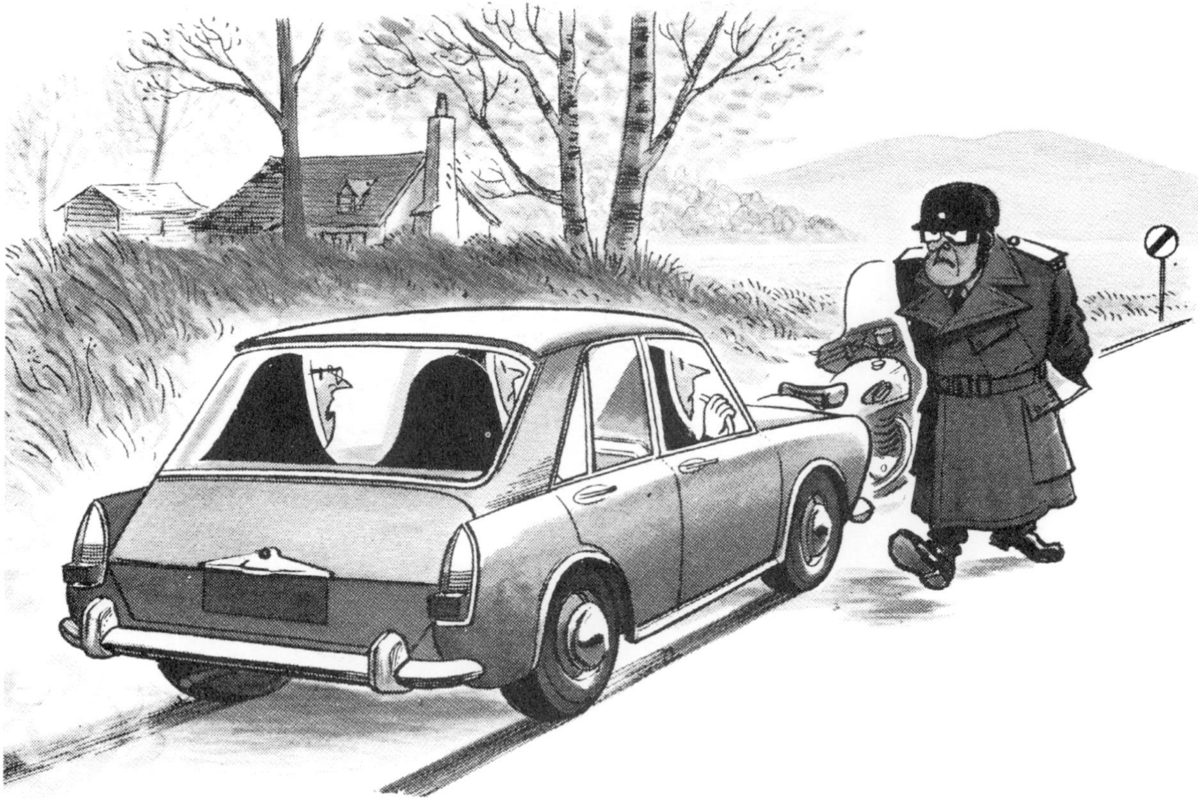

'Well, Sisters – what errand of mercy are you scorching to *this* time?

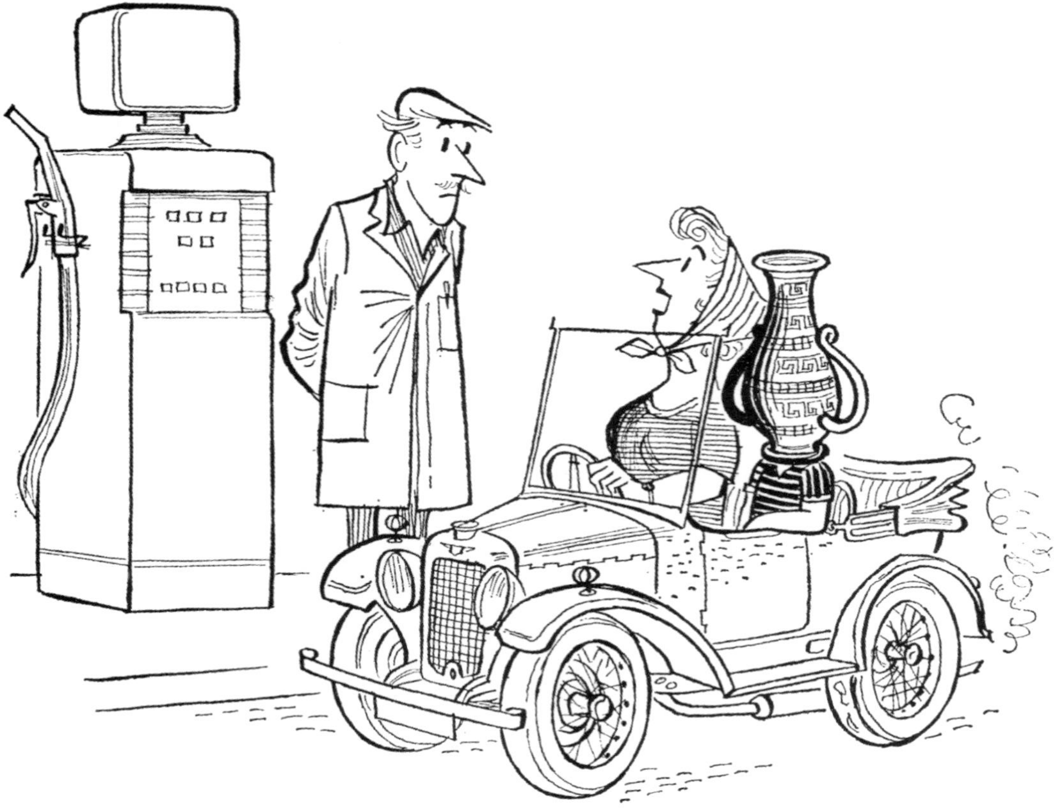

‘Two gallons, please, and some of that special oil that undoes rusty nuts!’

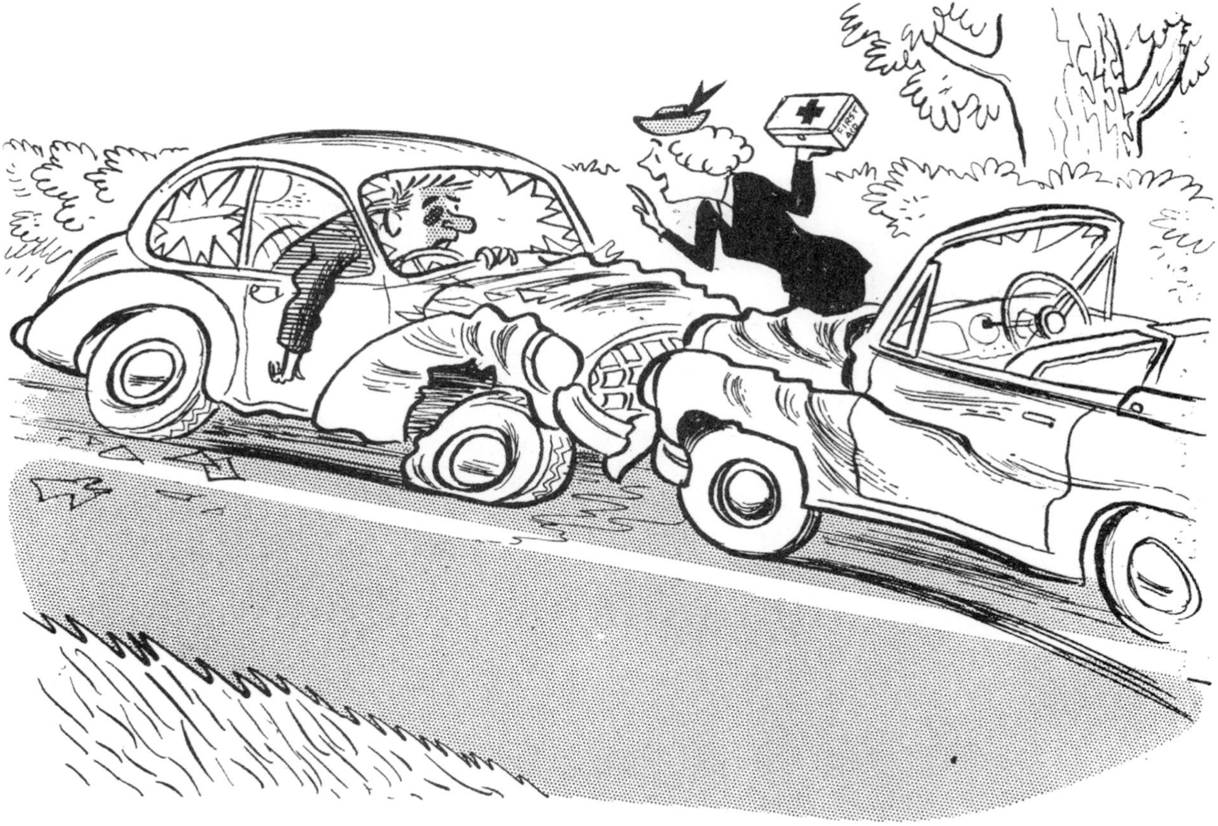
FIRST AID

'What a bit of luck for you, I'm a nurse!'

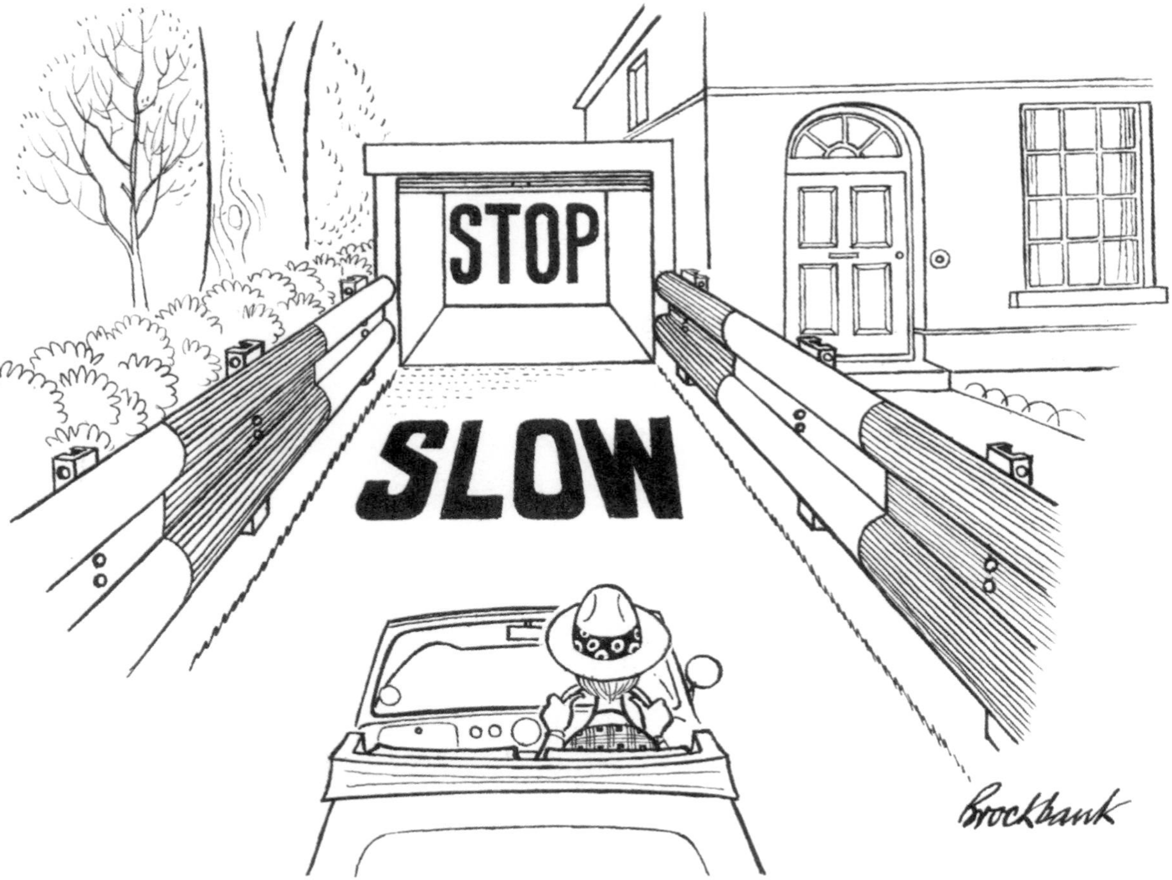
STOP
SLOW
Brockbank

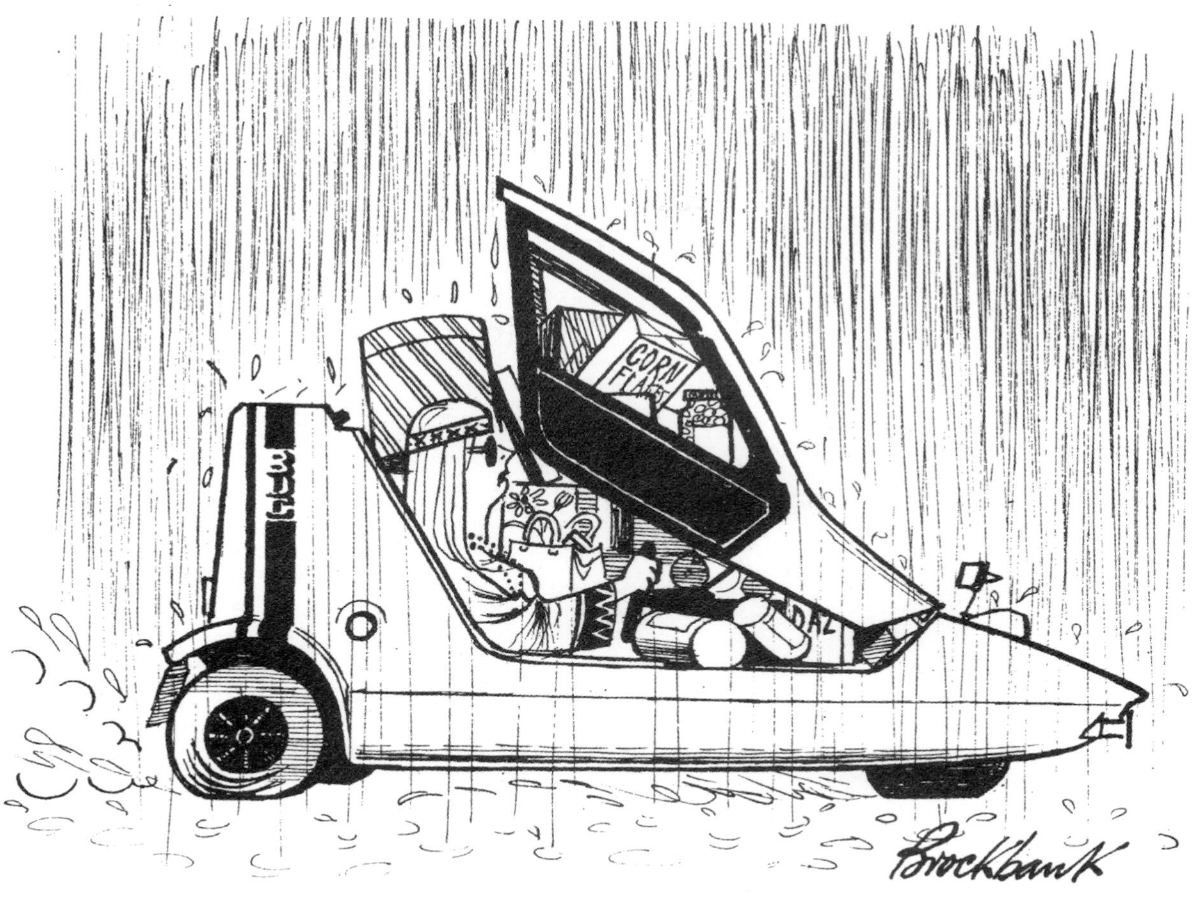
CORN
DAZ
Brockbank

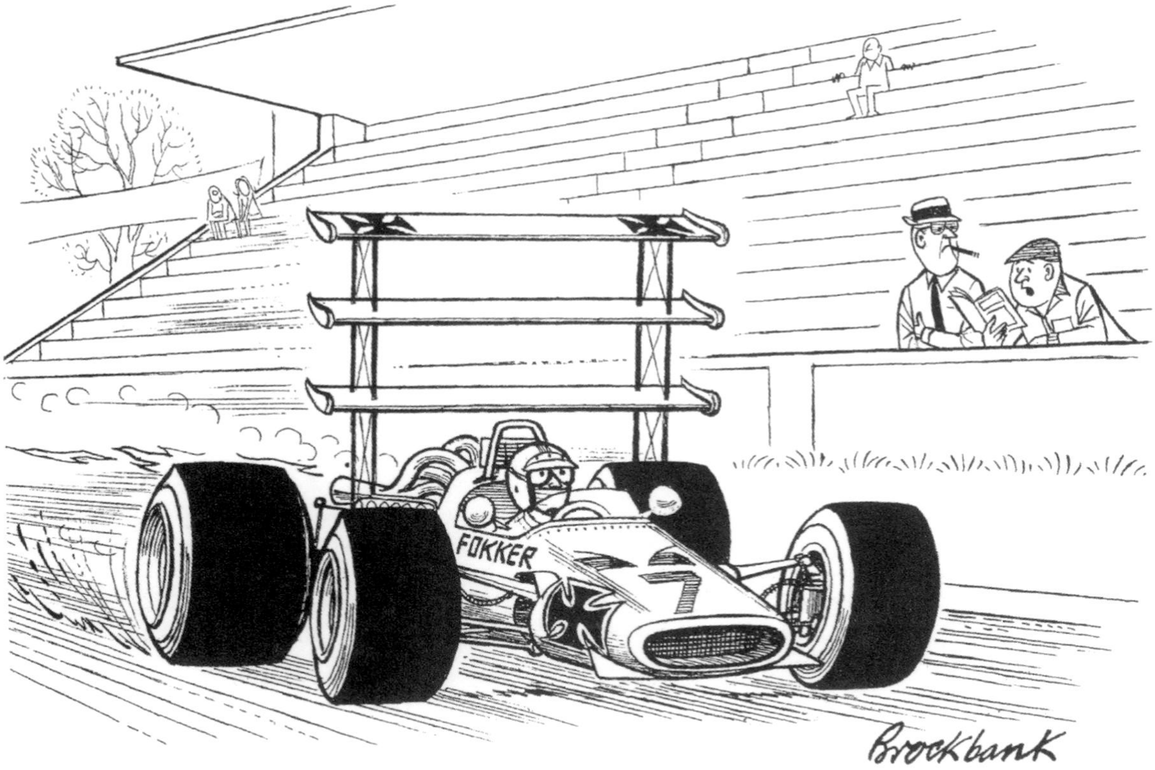
FOKKER
Brockbank

‘Manufacturer: Fokker. Driver: Baron von Richtofen’

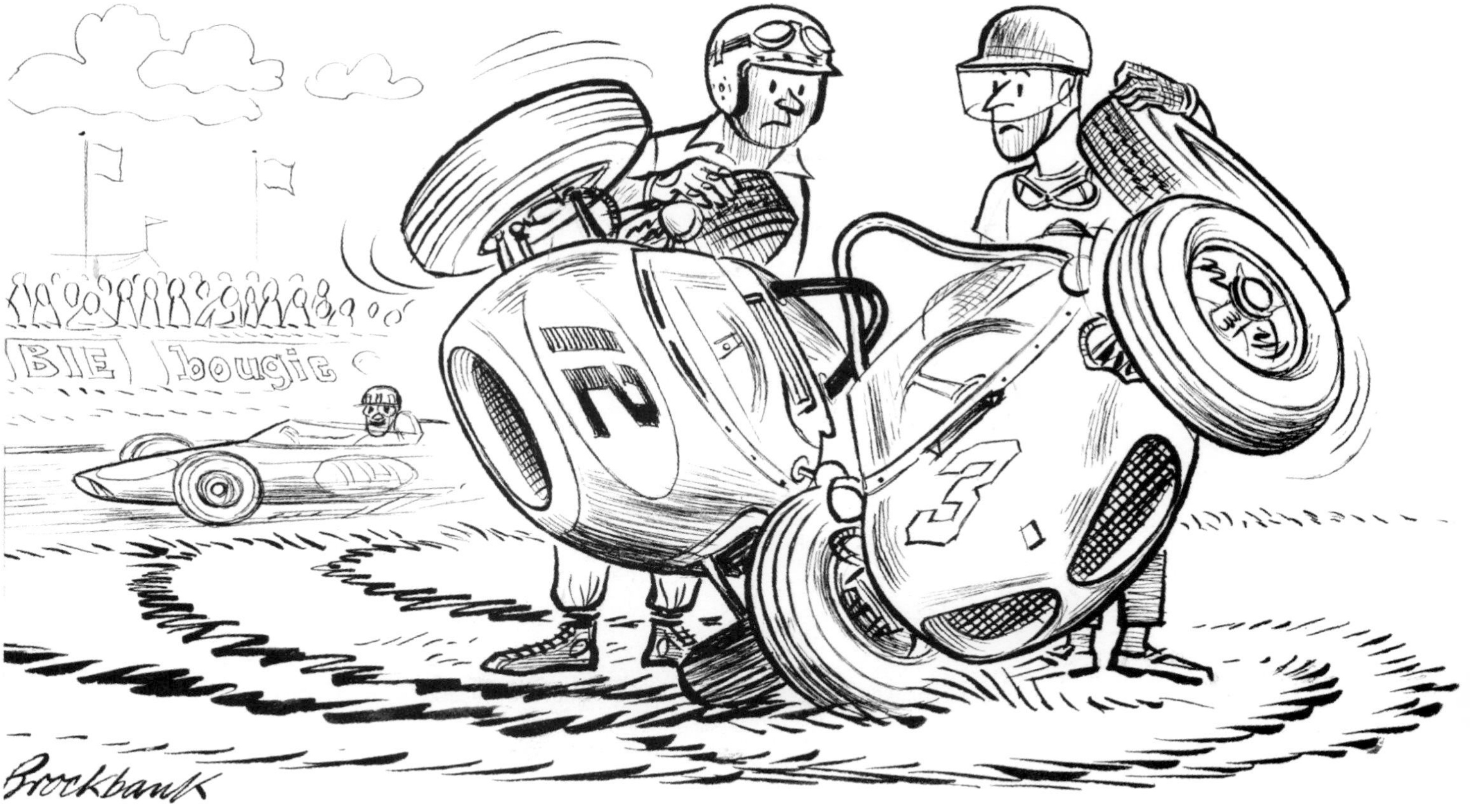
BIE
bougie
Brockbank

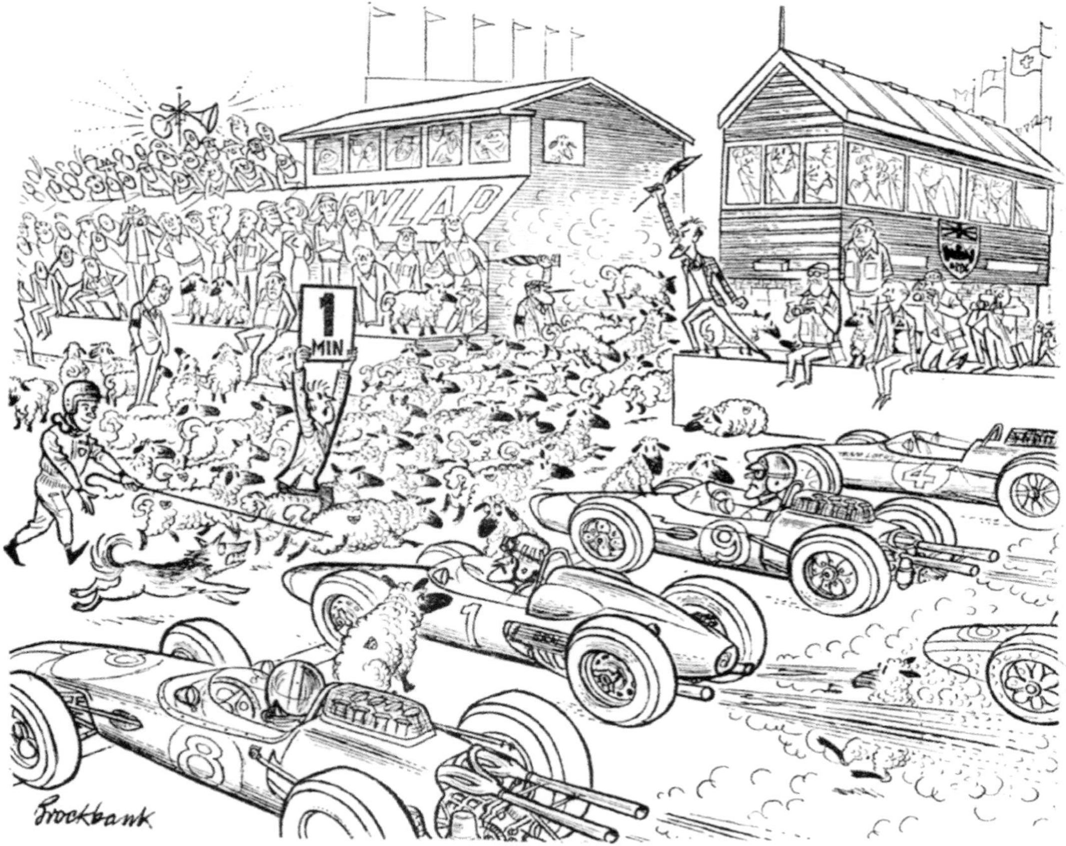
1
MIN
Brockbank

Jimmy Clark rounding up the Silverstone sheep

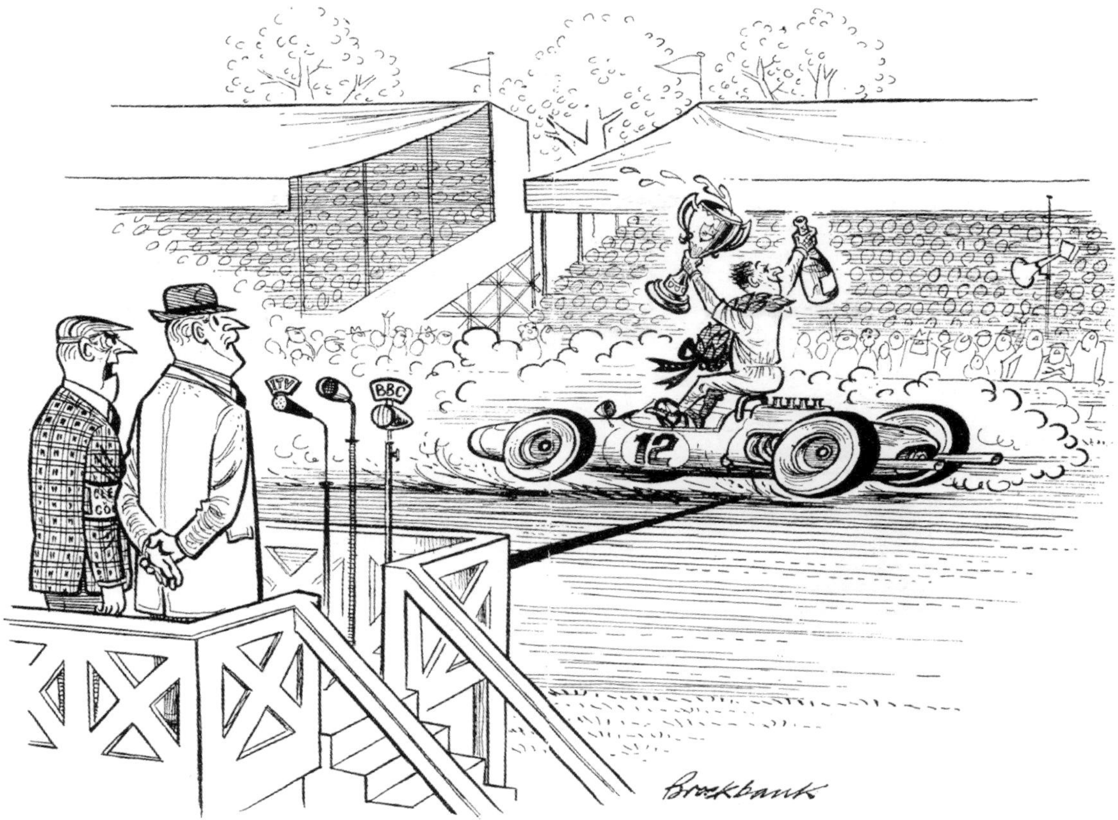
ITV
BBC
12
Brockbank

‘In this particular case it might have been wiser to have the champagne *after* the lap of honour.’

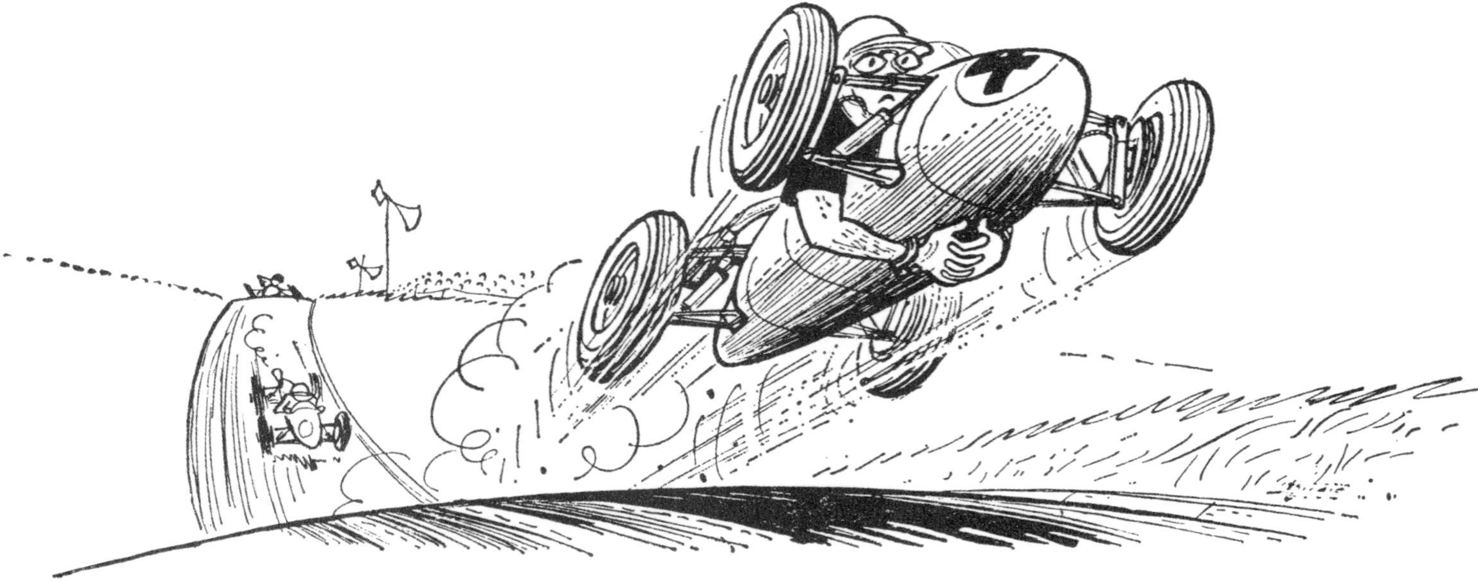

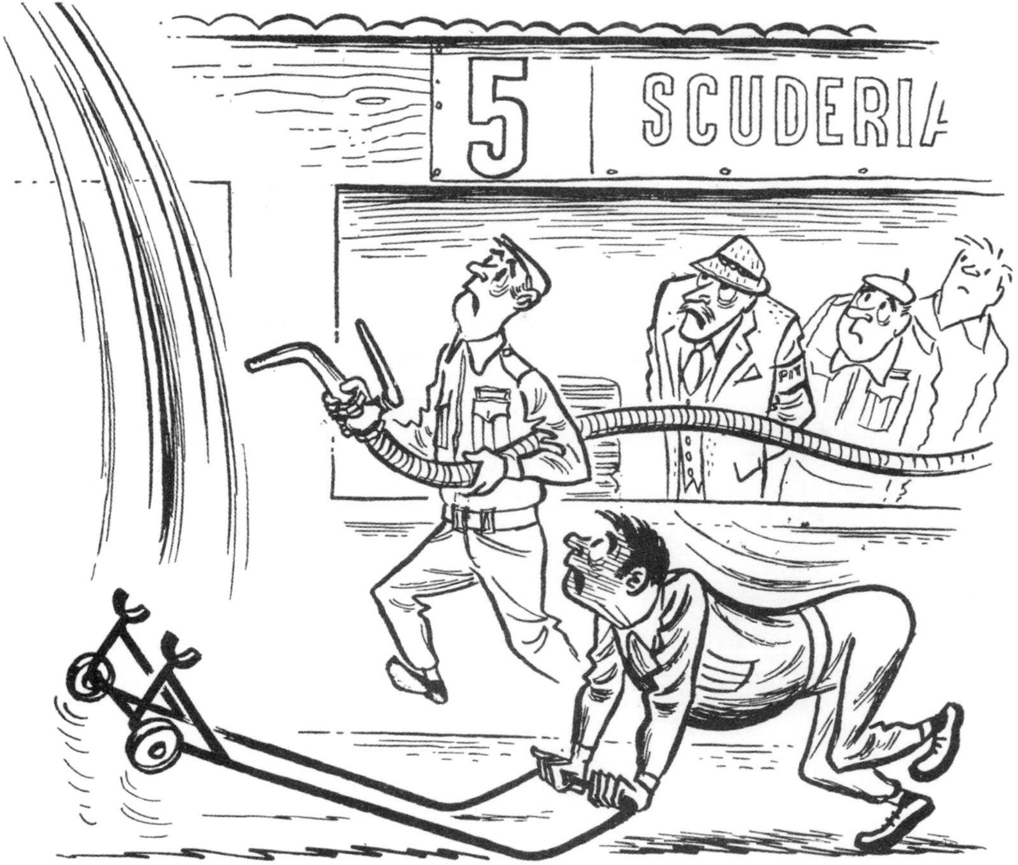
5
SCUDERIA
PIT

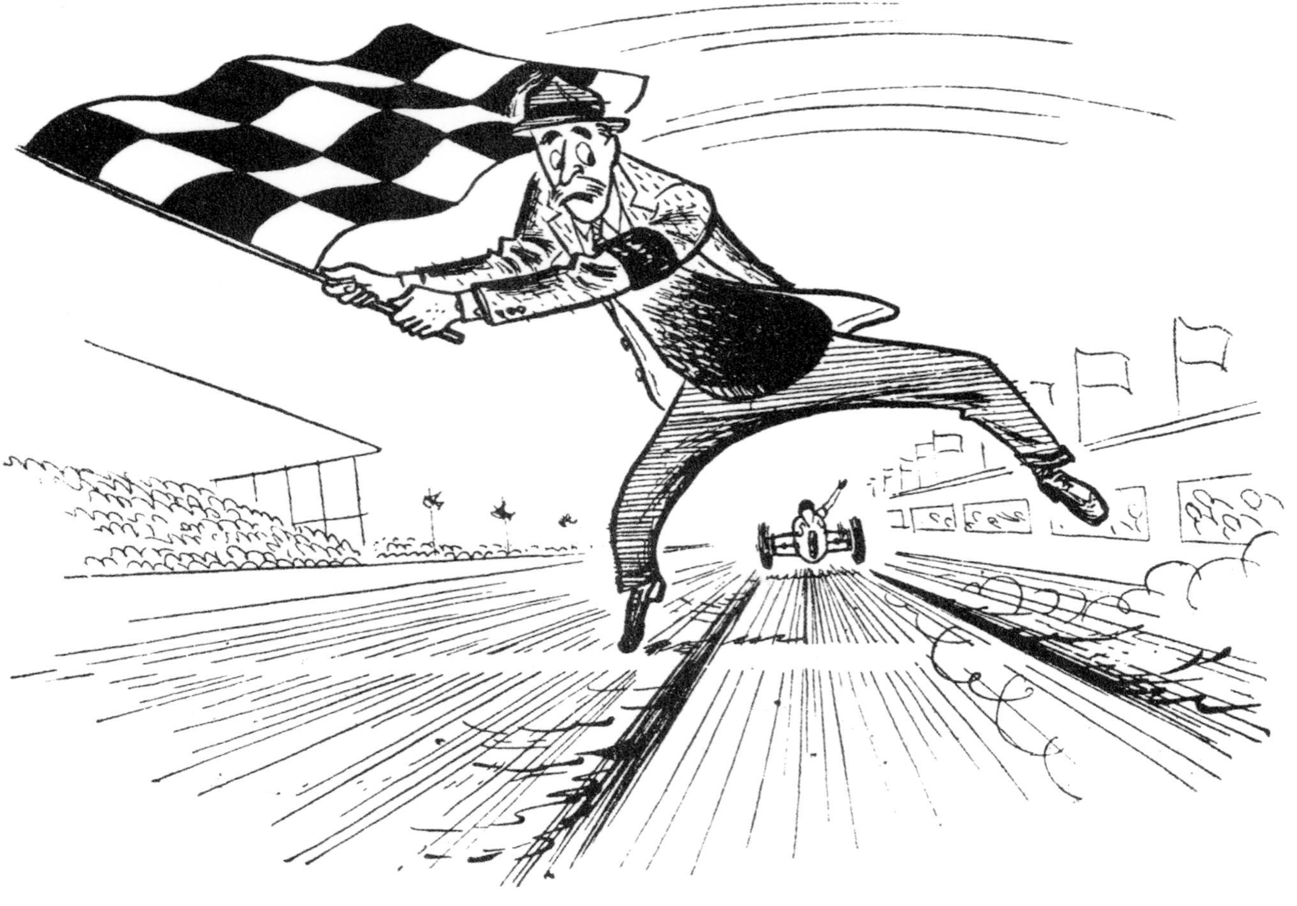

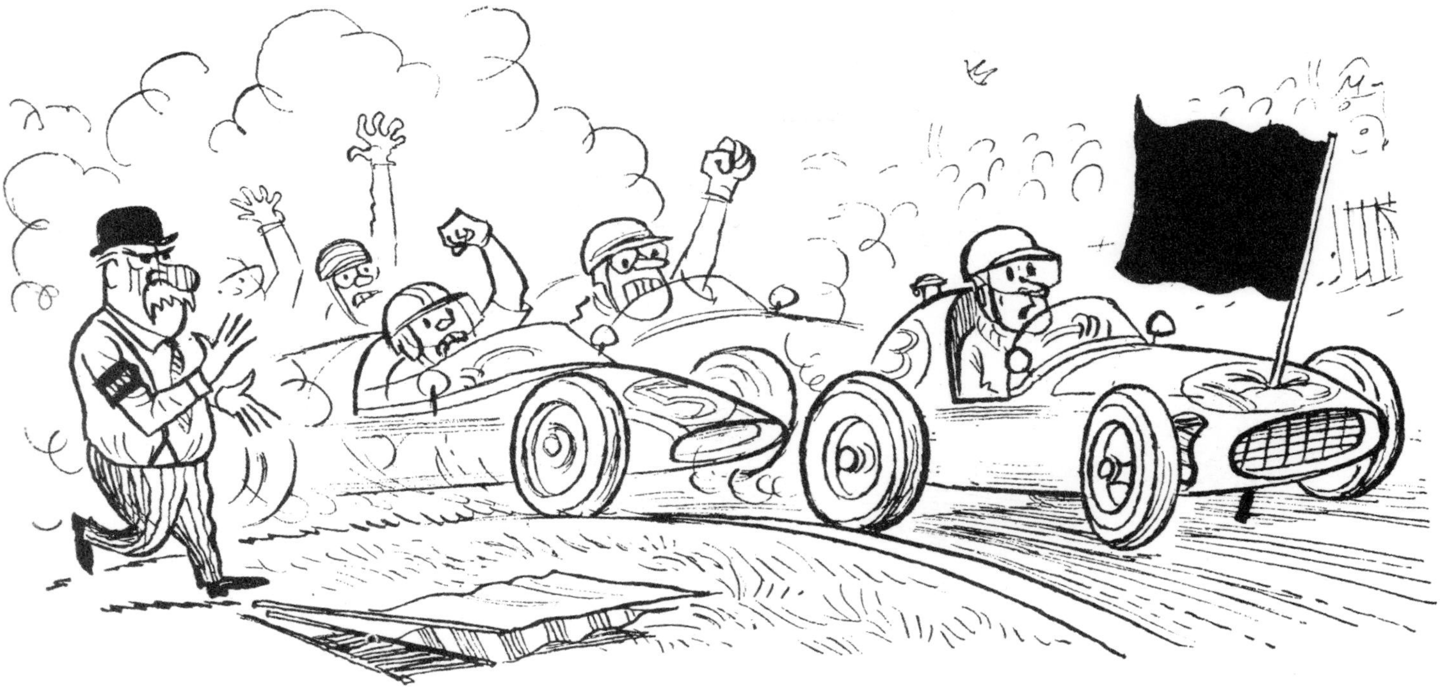

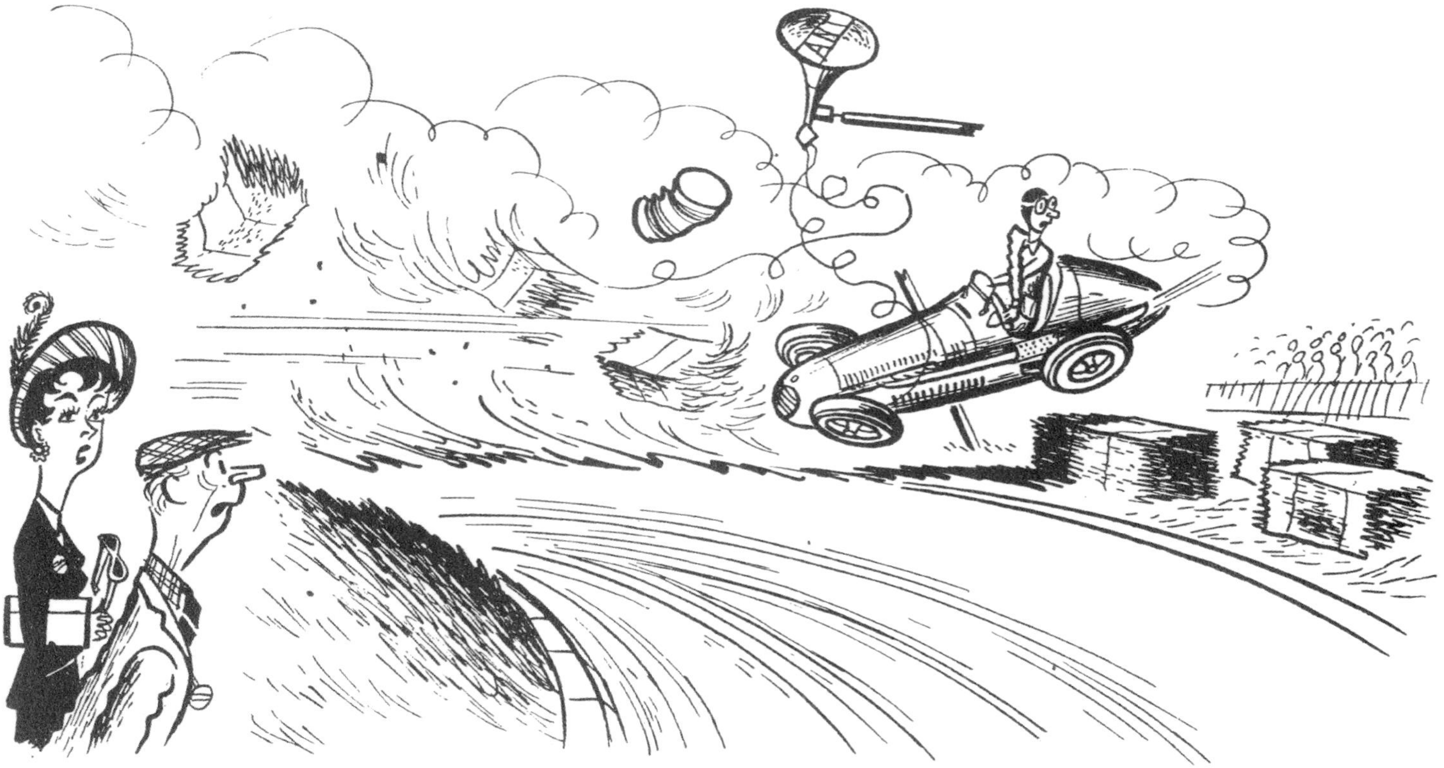

‘Do you mean they actually get *paid* for doing that?’

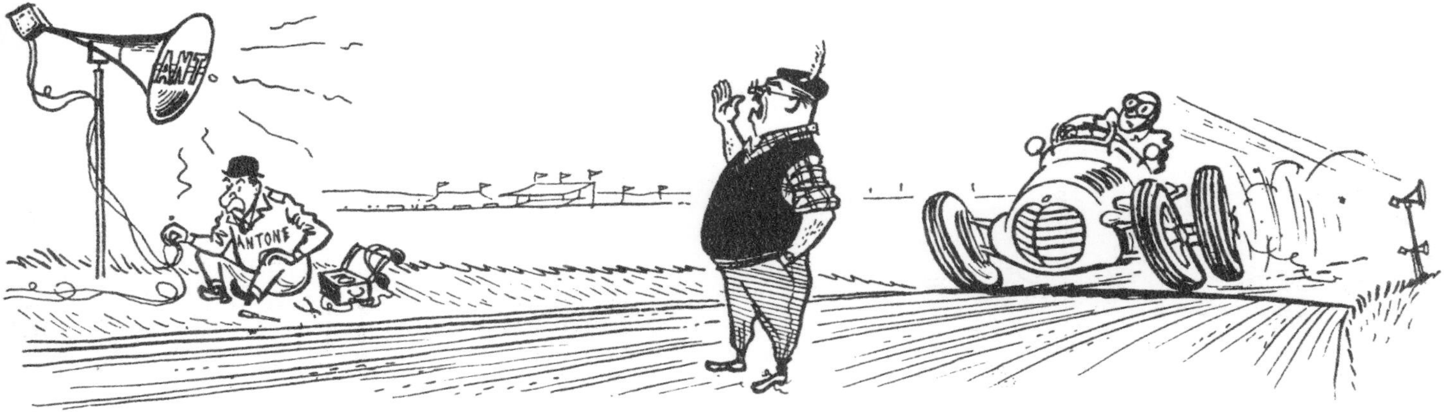
ANTONE

'All I can hear is a high-pitched scream rising in pitch.'

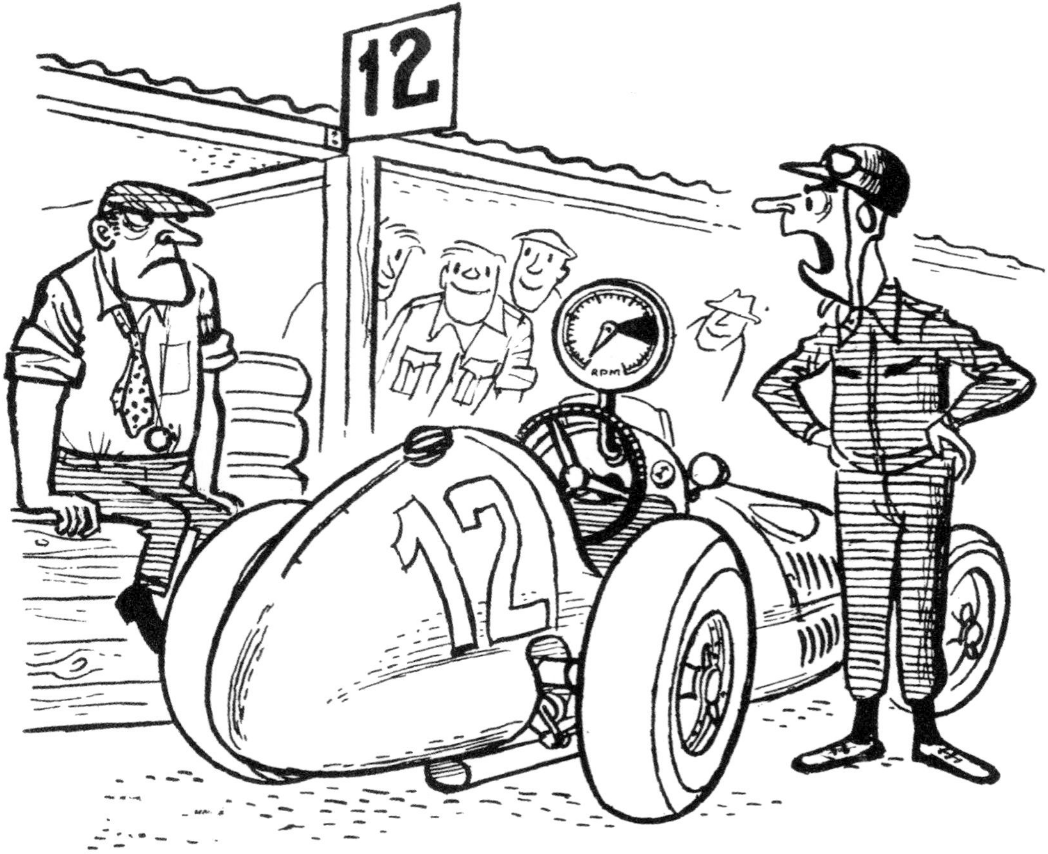
12
12
RPM

'I've had enough of your thinly veiled insults.'

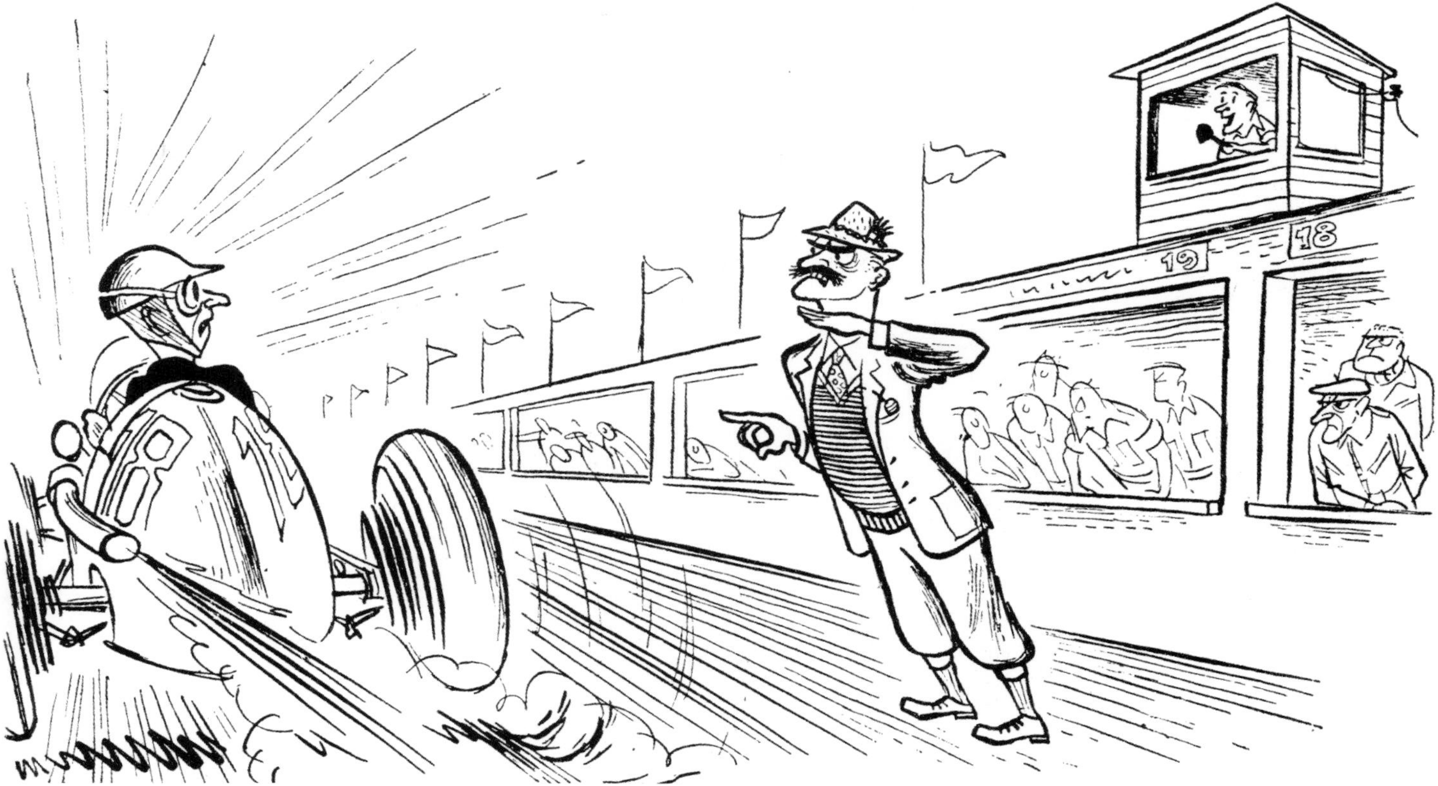
18
19
18

'No. 18 has just been given the "Flat Out" signal.'

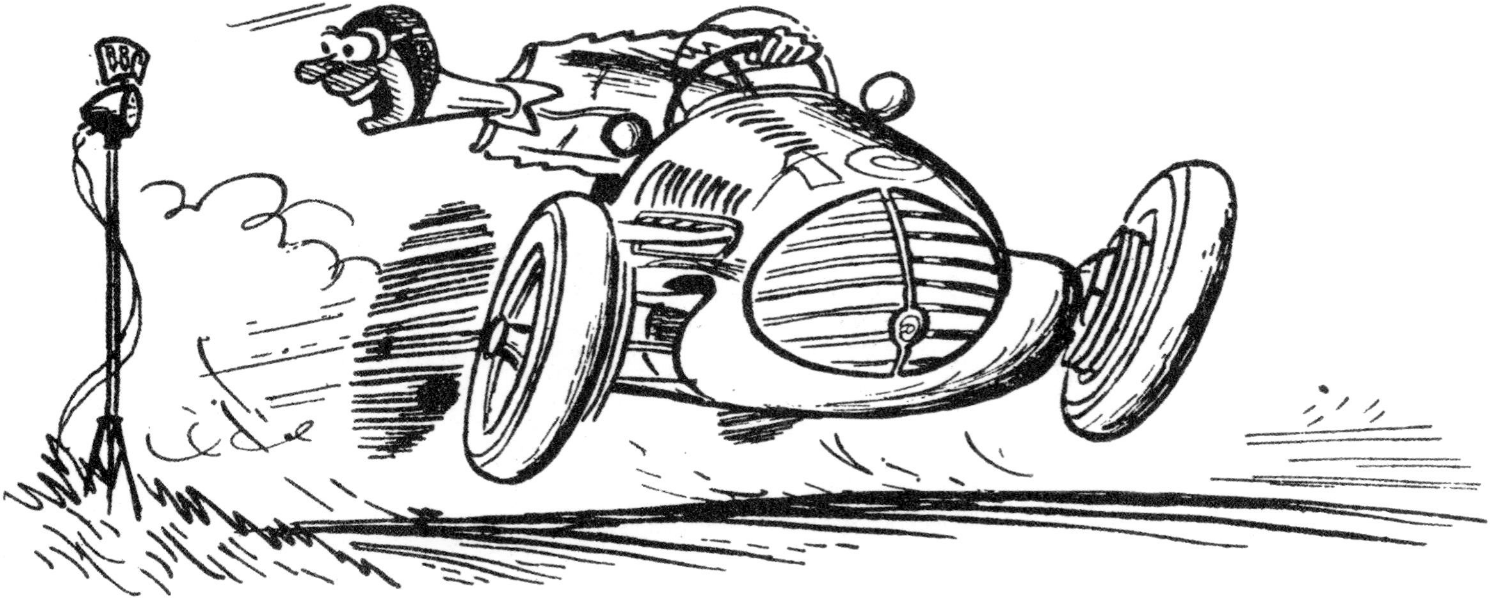
BBC

'Hello, Mom and Dad and all at home!'

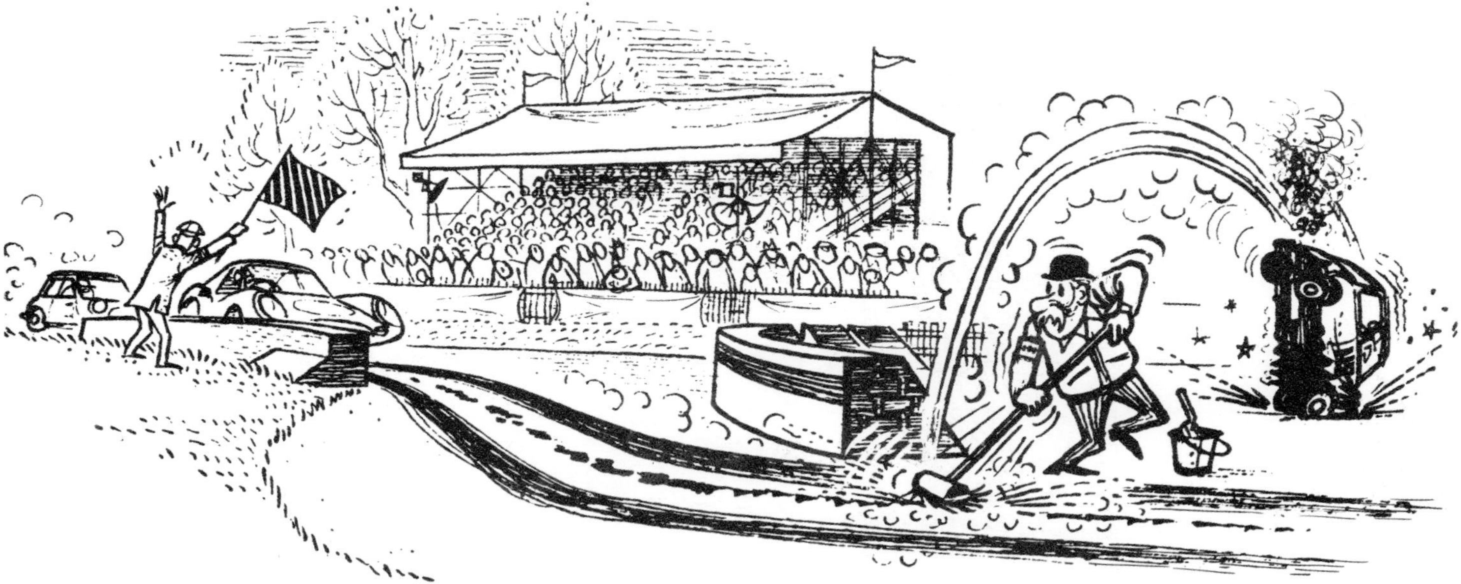

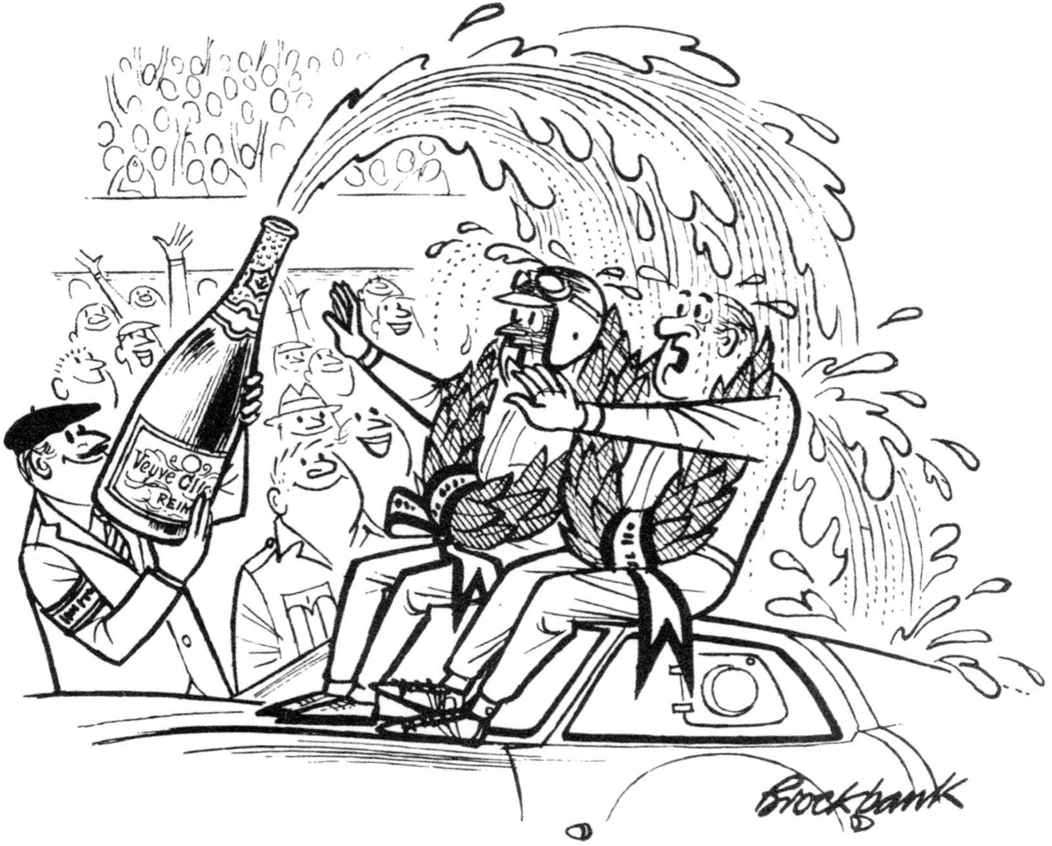
Brockbank

‘No, no – we never touch the stuff.’

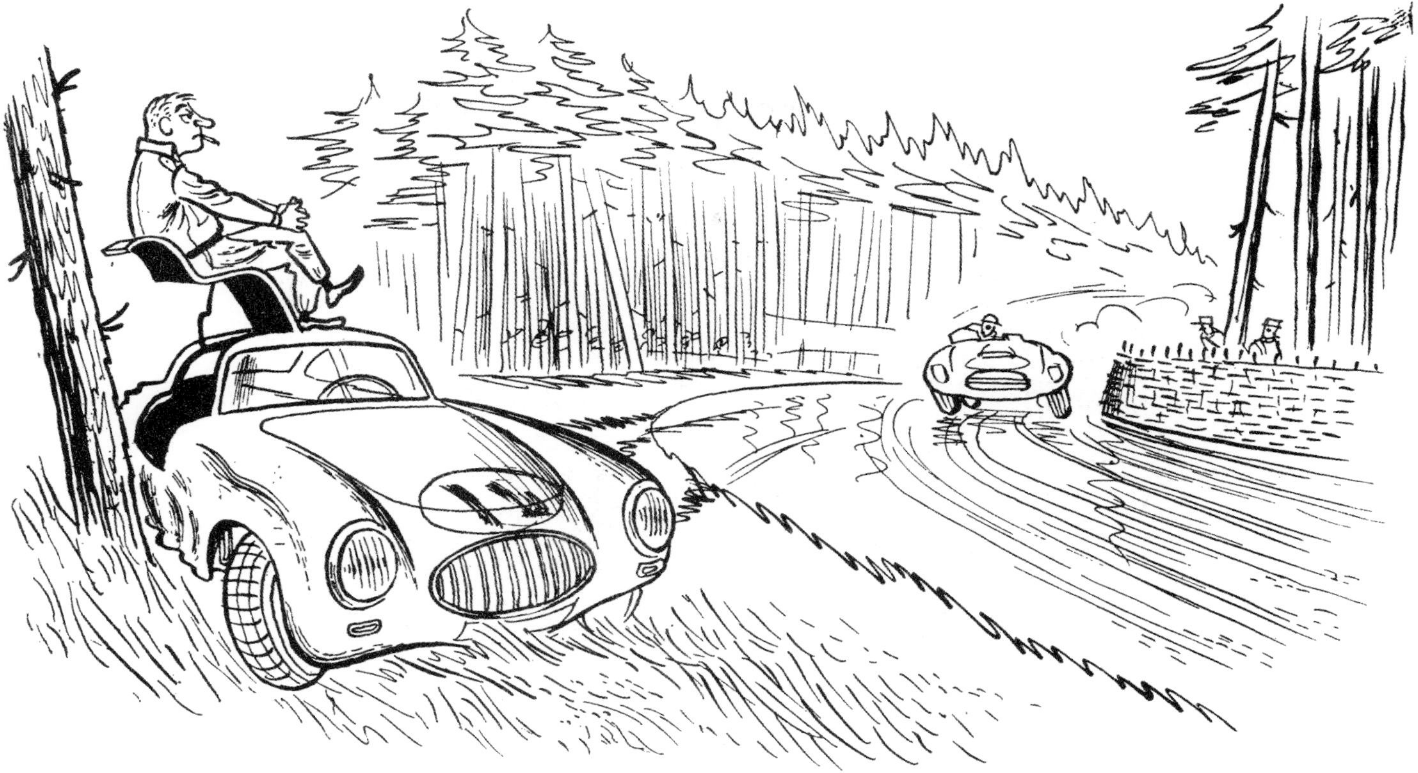

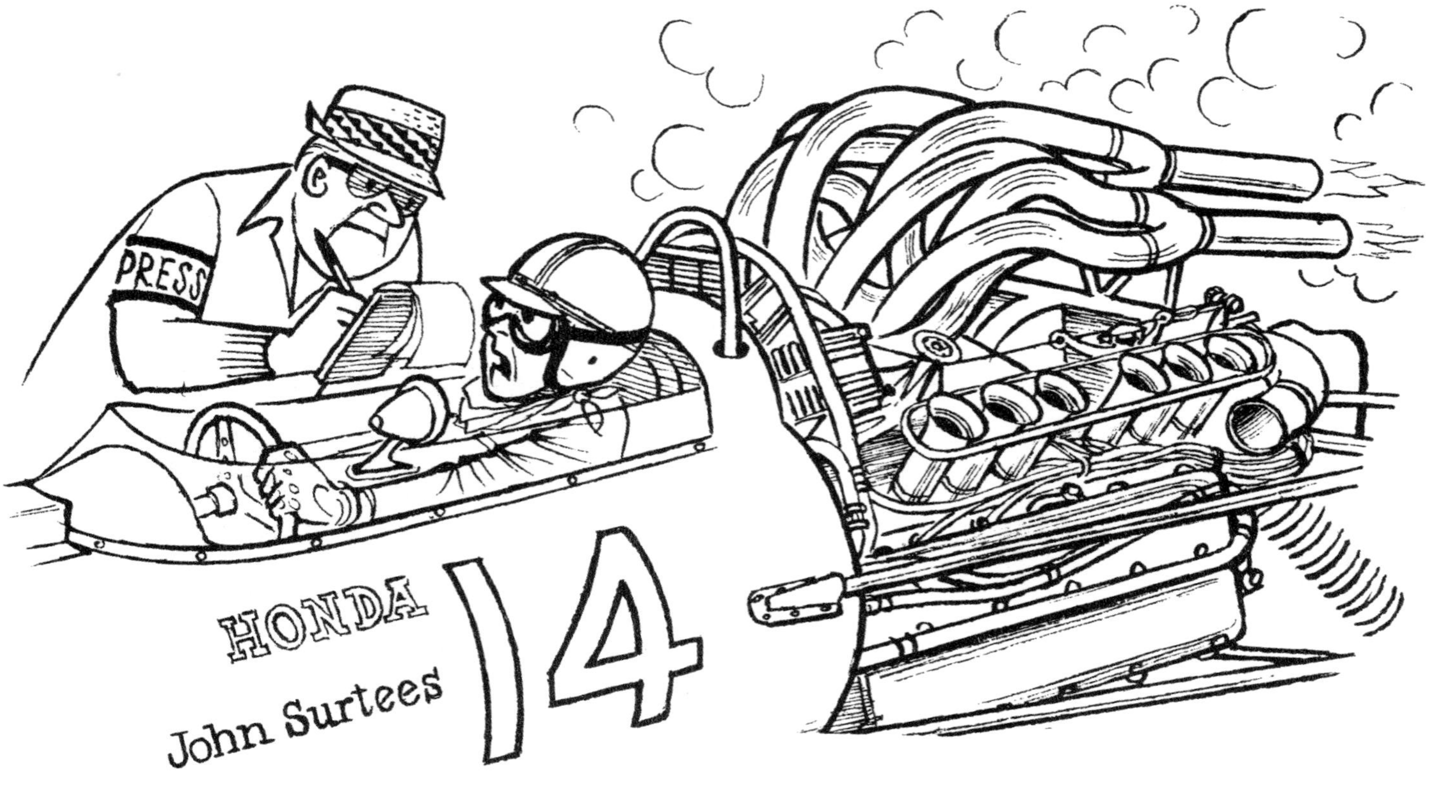
PRESS
HONDA
John Surtees
14

'Before all this I led a relatively peaceful life, racing motor-cycles.'

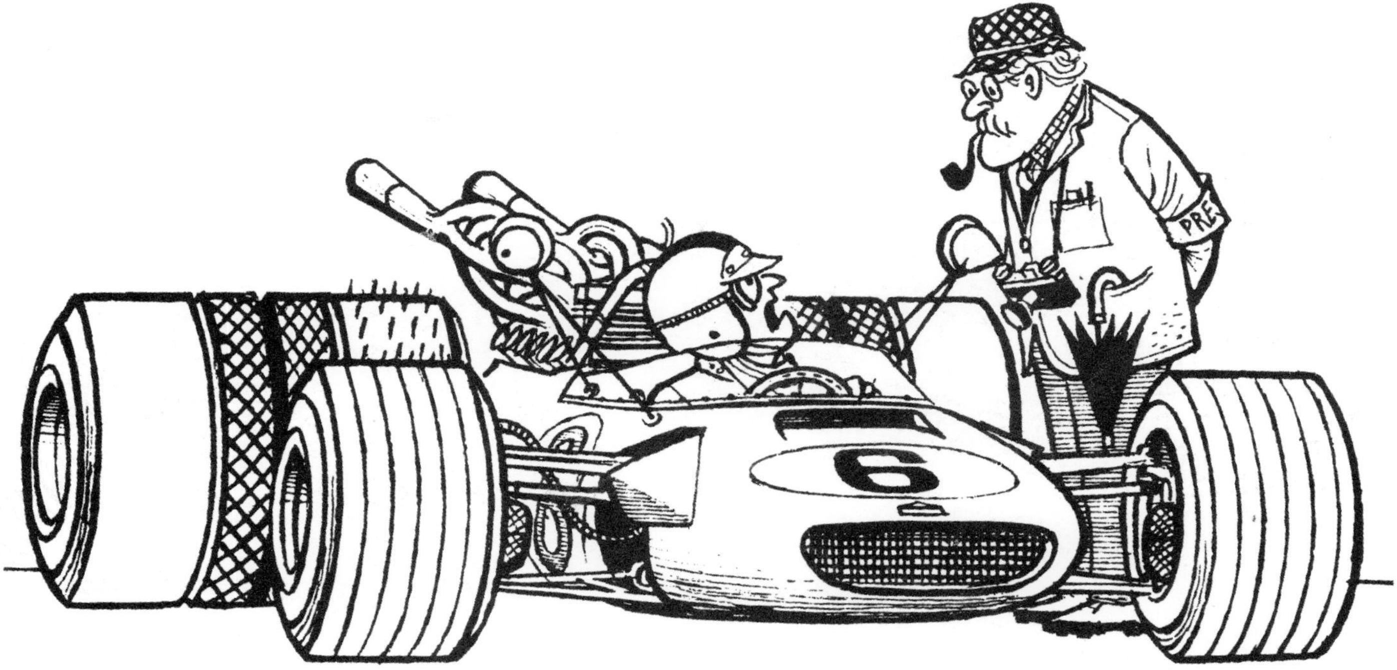
PRE
PRE
6

‘From now on I don’t give a damn whether it rains, shines or snows.’

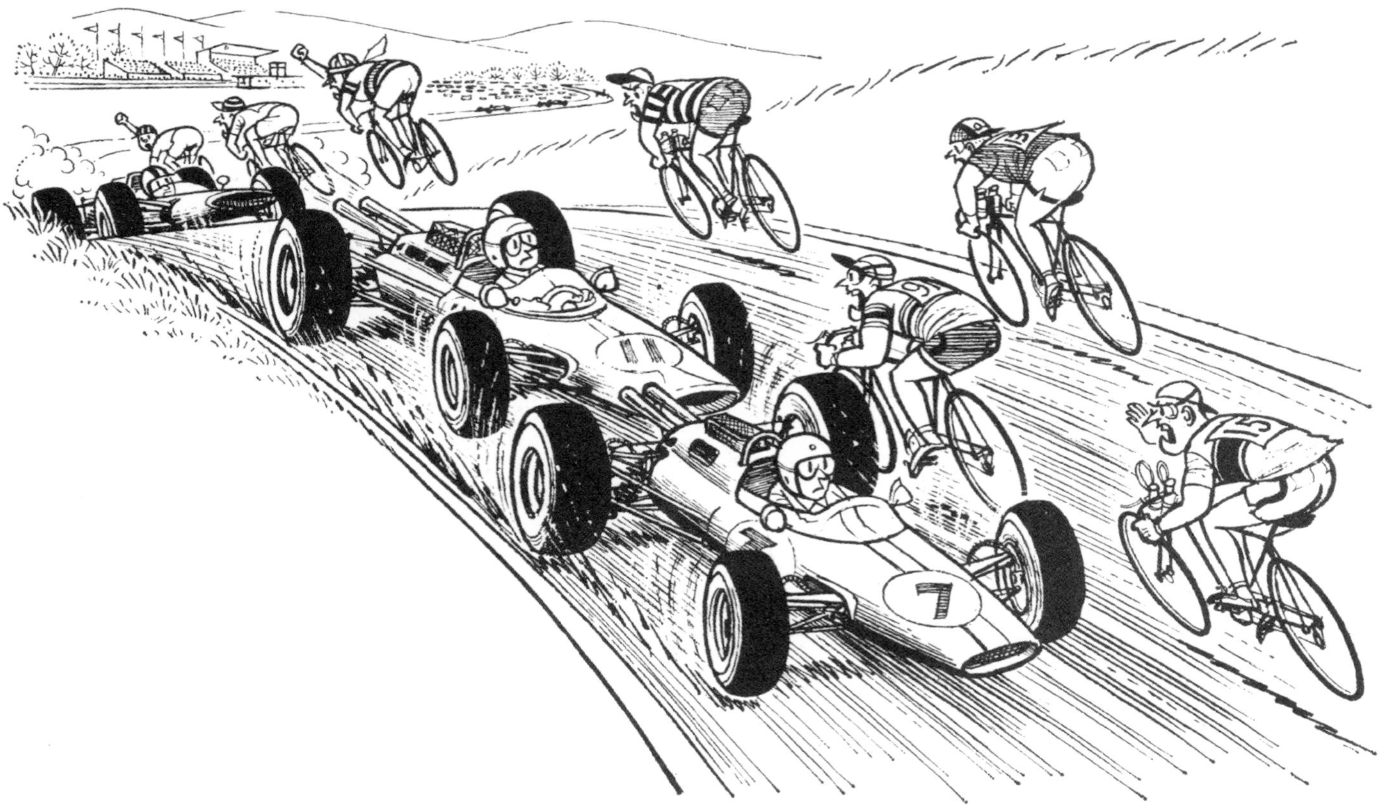
7

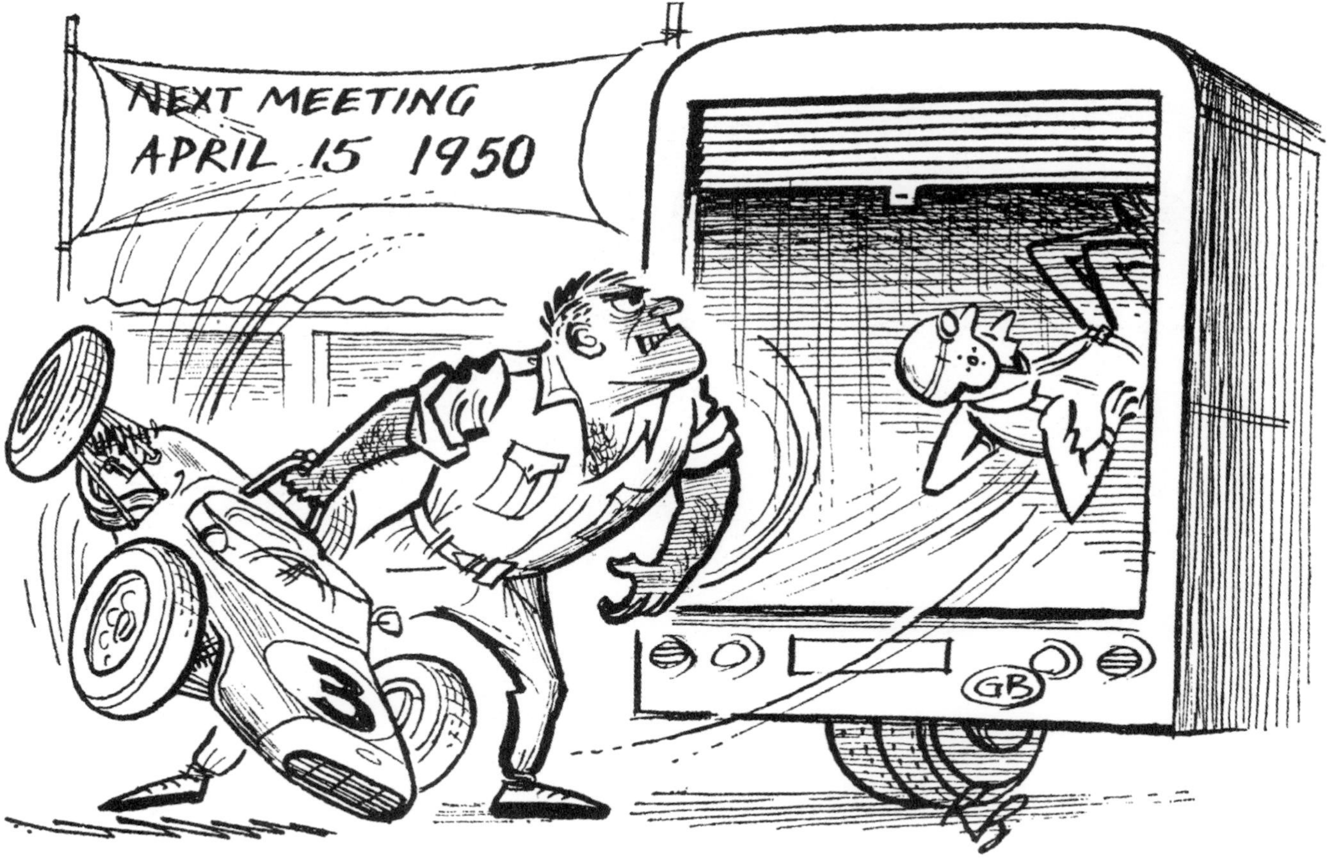
NEXT MEETING
APRIL 15 1950
3
GB

End of the Season

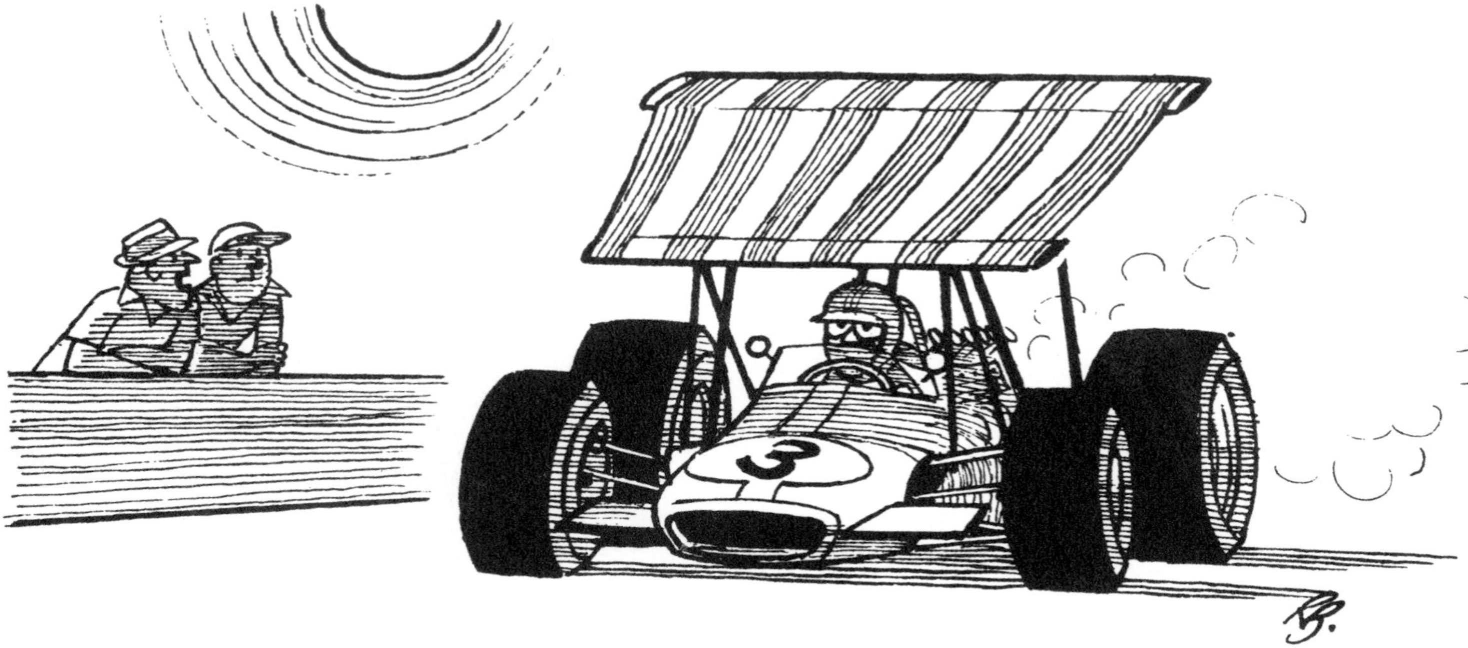
3

'He was determined to play this Monaco cool.'

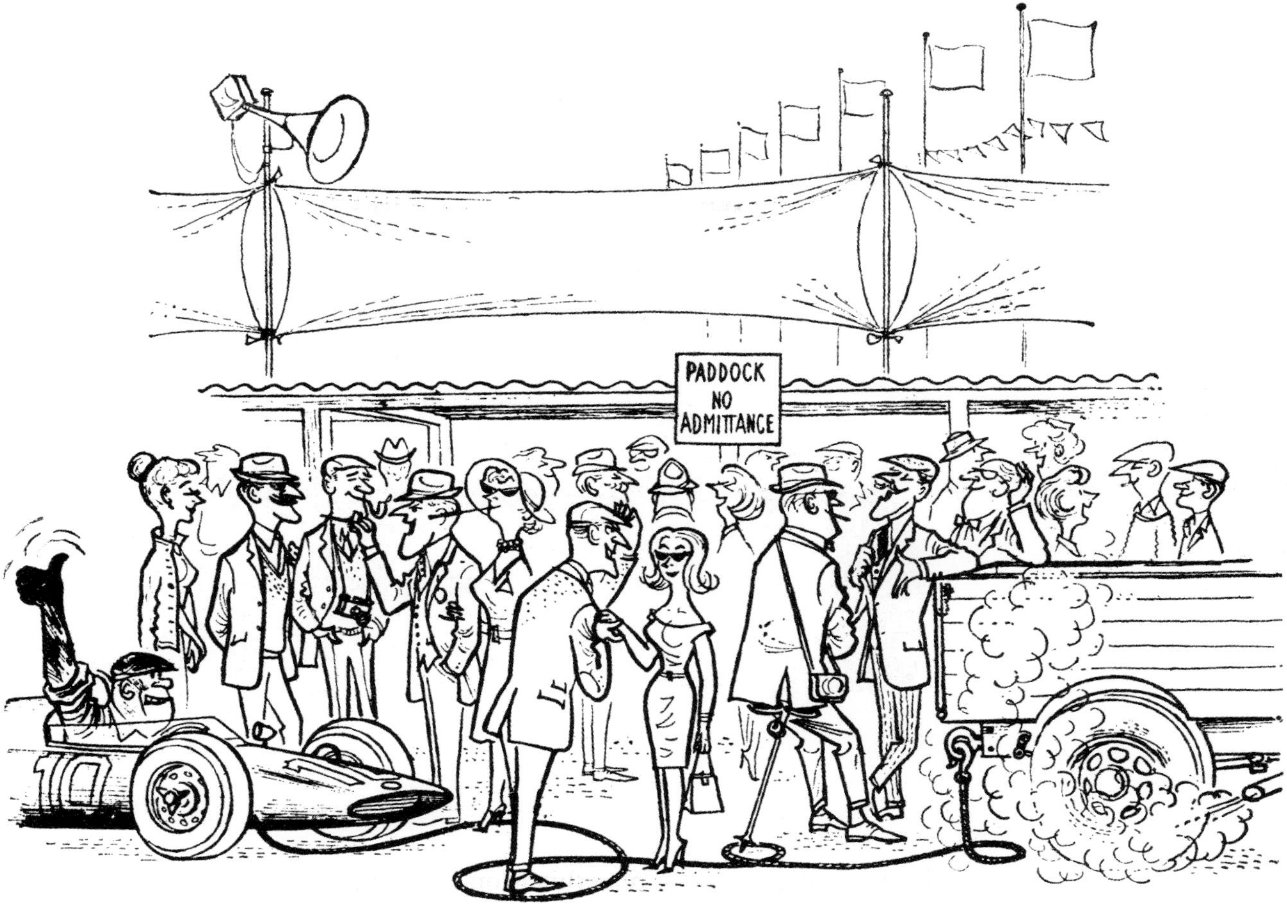
PADDOCK
NO
ADMITTANCE
10

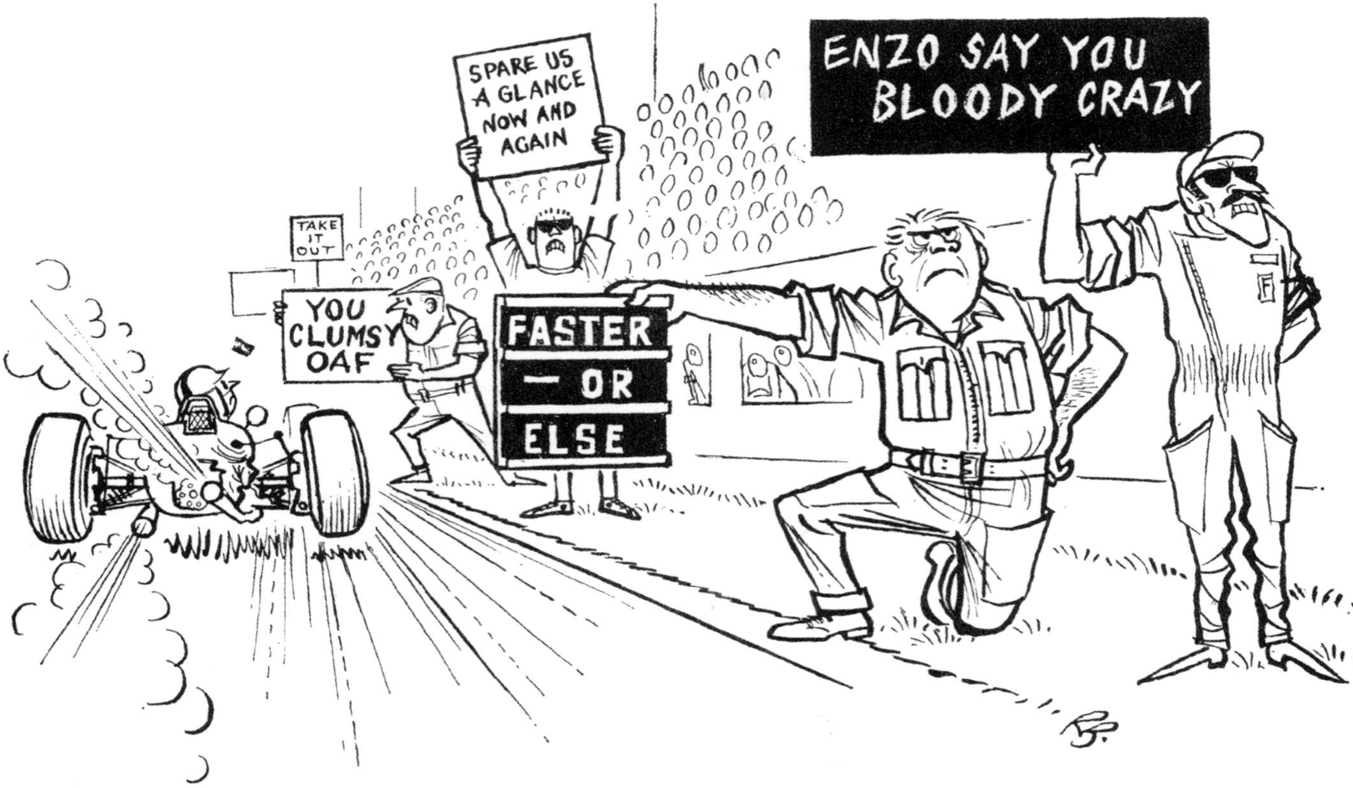
ENZO SAY YOU BLOODY CRAZY
SPARE US A GLANCE NOW AND AGAIN
TAKE IT OUT
YOU CLUMSY OAF
FASTER — OR ELSE

All pit signals to be 'in clear' rather than by secret code, so that spectators are 'in the picture' at all times.

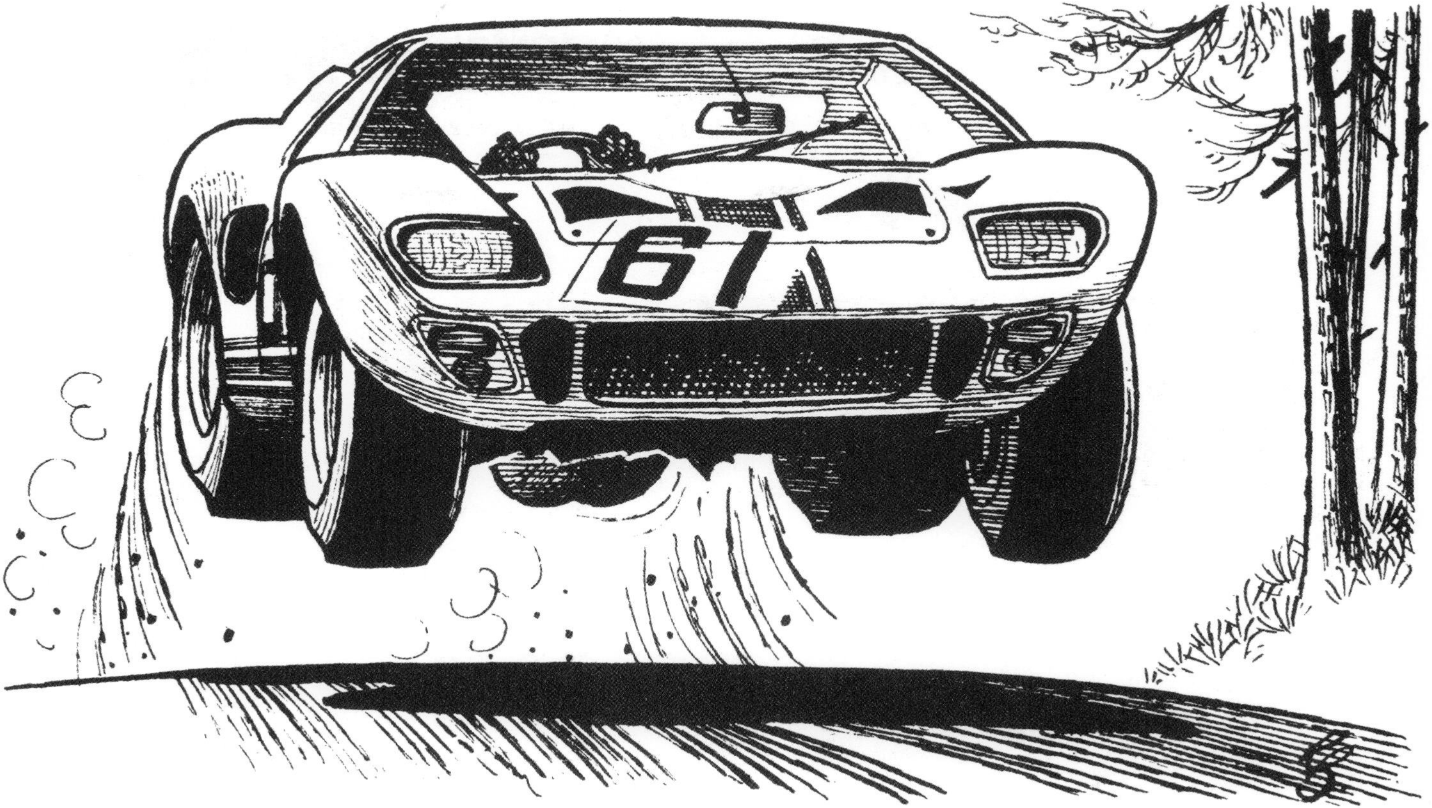
61

‘With only two hours to go, No. 61 has a comfortable lead.’

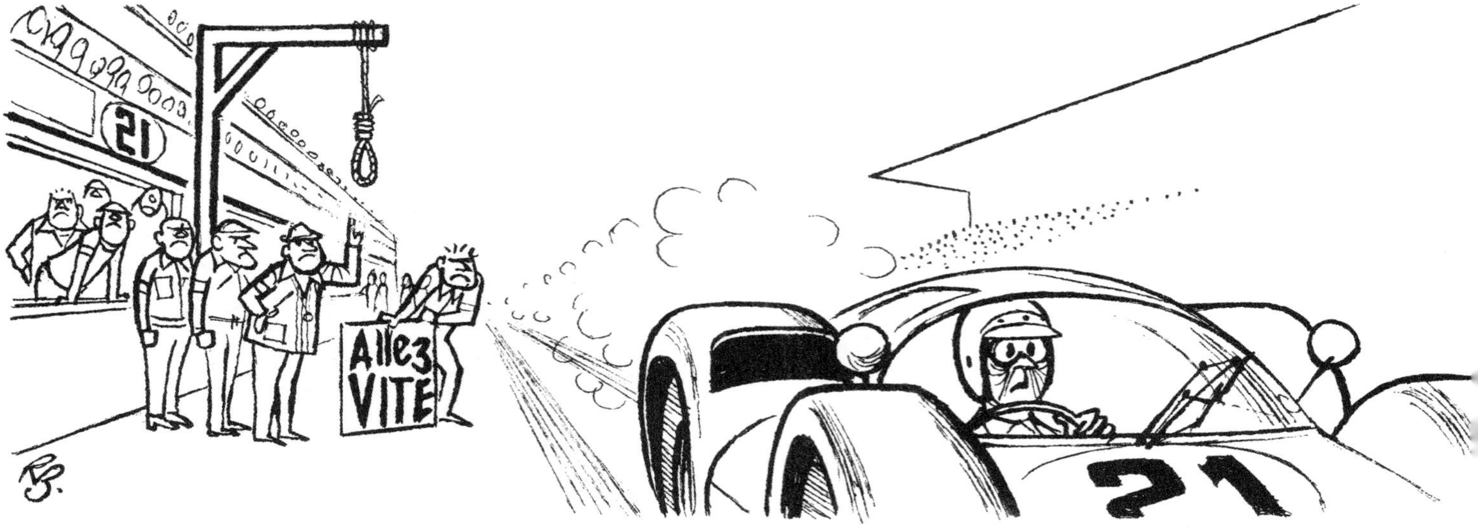
21
Allez
VITE
21

'If there is one thing a driver appreciates it is up-do-date information from his Pit.'

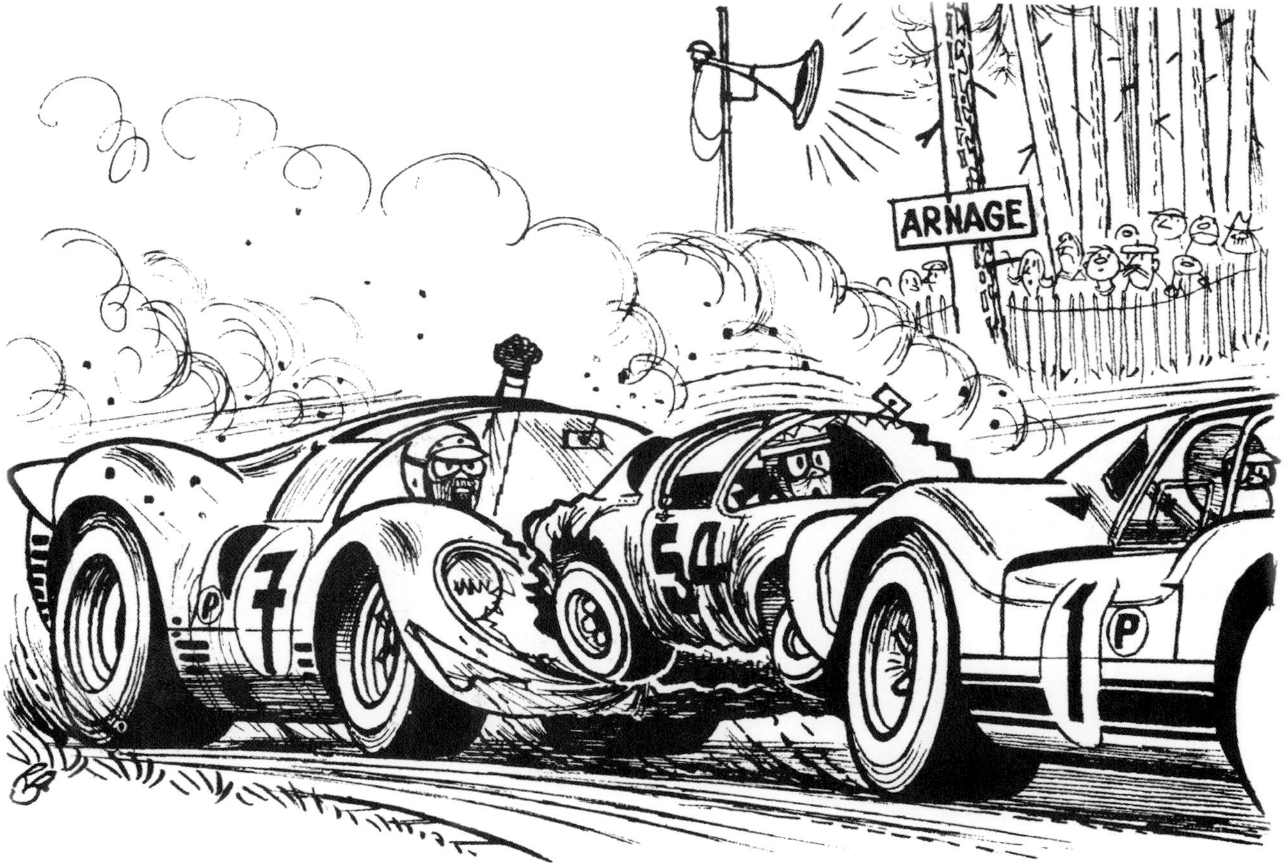
ARNAGE
7
54
1

'Fantastic news! Car No. 54 has pulverized the 1100cc class record with a lap at no less than 132 miles per hour!'

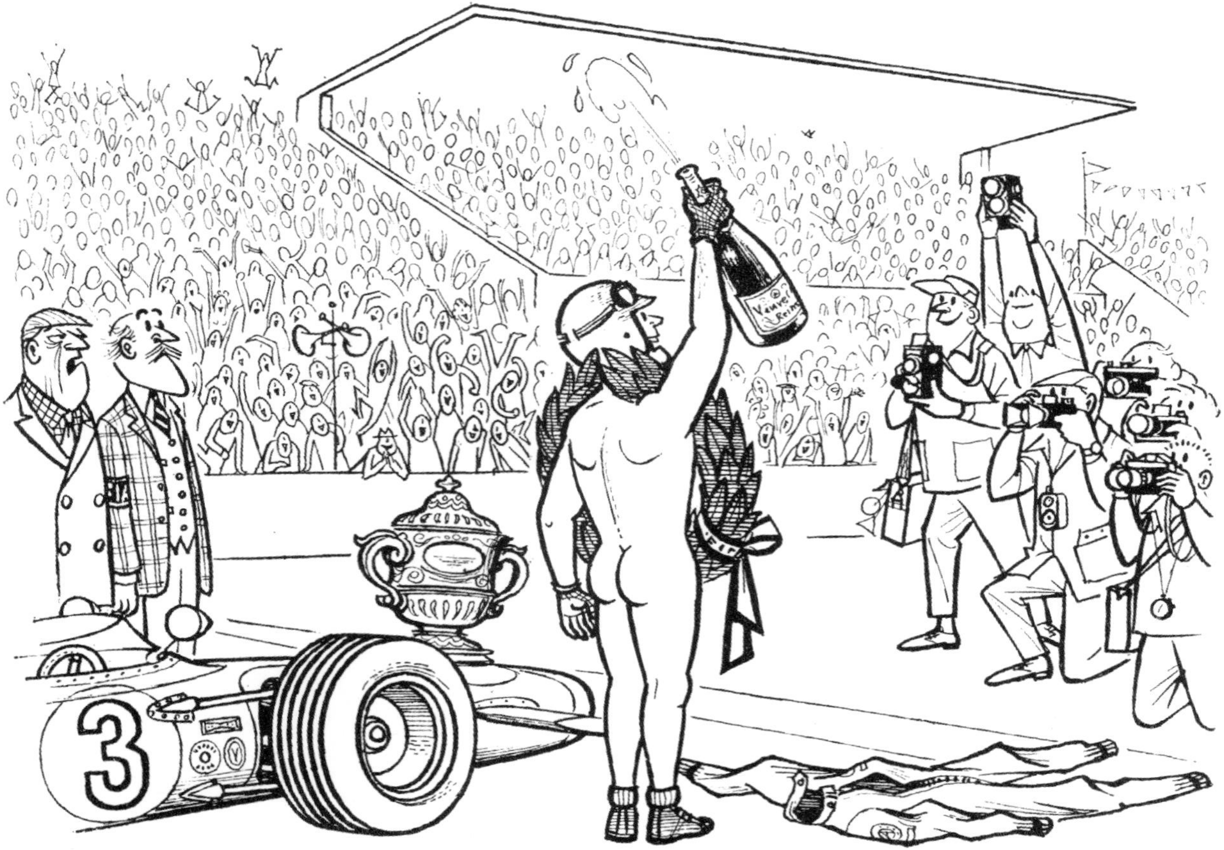
3

'Another first in the Entertainment game!'